جماليـة الغيـب

POEMS FROM
IQBAL

POEMS FROM
IQBAL

RENDERINGS IN ENGLISH VERSE
WITH COMPARATIVE URDU TEXT

Translated by
V.G. KIERNAN

OXFORD
UNIVERSITY PRESS

OXFORD
UNIVERSITY PRESS

Great Clarendon Street, Oxford OX2 6DP

Oxford University Press is a department of the University of Oxford.
It furthers the University's objective of excellence in research, scholarship,
and education by publishing worldwide in

Oxford New York

Auckland Cape Town Dar es Salaam Hong Kong Karachi
Kuala Lumpur Madrid Melbourne Mexico City Nairobi
New Delhi Shanghai Taipei Toronto

with offices in

Argentina Austria Brazil Chile Czech Republic France Greece
Guatemala Hungary Italy Japan Poland Portugal Singapore
South Korea Switzerland Turkey Ukraine Vietnam

Oxford is a registered trade mark of Oxford University Press
in the UK and in certain other countries

First published 1955

Published in 1999 by Oxford University Press
by arrangement with Iqbal Academy Pakistan.
Reprinted by permission of John Murray (Publishers) Ltd.

ISBN 978-0-19-579974-3

Fourth Impression 2009

This Edition with a new Preface by Oxford University Press, 2004

Typeset in Times (English)
Typeset in Noori Nastaliq (Urdu)
Cover Design by K.B. Abro

Printed in Pakistan at
Mehran Printers, Karachi.
Published by
Ameena Saiyid, Oxford University Press
No. 38, Sector 15, Korangi Industrial Area, PO Box 8214
Karachi-74900, Pakistan.

CONTENTS

PART III.   ZARB-I-KALIM   The Rod of Moses

(Islam and the Muslim)

(Education and Culture)

(Woman)

PART IV.   ARMAGHAN-I-HEJAZ   The Gift of Hejaz

PART V.   PYAM-I-MASHRIQ   The Message of the East

PREFACE TO THE 2004 EDITION

In the three-quarters of a century since Muhammad Iqbal's death he has lost none of his stature as one of the last great poets of his part of the world. We must hope that he will not prove to have been the *last* great poet bred by his native soil, a fading away too frequent in some other latitudes or longitudes.

This selection from his poems, translated into English verse, was as its second edition, revised and brought out in London in 1955. The original texts were chosen from Iqbal's Urdu poems, native to northern Indian with a few picked out for me from his more copious output in Persian, a language which shares a good deal of the same vocabulary. On his choice of languages, Iqbal Singh's book should be pondered; Iqbal was fluent in both. To me it now seems less likely that he chose Persian the most often in order to appeal to a wider, more cosmopolitan audience—as I suggested formerly,—and more likely that he found it easier, more restful to write in Persian, with its lyrical romantic character. Urdu on the other hand, half Hindi, brought him face to face with the real, intransigent problems of the day, of which the hardest, the future of the Punjab, was to prove insoluble except by violence.

His Urdu poems are even today still vibrant with the spirit of a new age, of hurrying movement, of dynamic effort. His message was that the time had come for action; that India, especially Muslim India—the commanding force during the many years of the Mughal era—had sunk for too long into sleepy routine. It was a message welcomed by the aspiring youth of all the communities. But in whatever manner the call for action might be hailed, the direction it was to take was much harder to foresee.

Often the poems reflect a complex personality, allowing glimpses of a good many of those doubts and contradictions to be found hidden in all of us. There was in them also the complexity of a time of changes, breaking in on a mode of living and thinking that had lain static or torpid for ages. Iqbal had penetrating insights into this tangled web, but he suffered from various impediments. He shows little knowledge of history, a subject very long neglected in India, in contrast with China or

Europe,—or of the new social sciences, like Economics. He could extol the Turkish peasant conscripts of the Great War as 'Defenders of the Faith', when they were really victims of a mouldering past, while a new future was being opened for their country by Kemal Ataturk.

To help in smoothing the way for progress he wrote—in English, increasingly in his day the language of educated Indians—a work on *The Reconstruction of Religious Thought in Islam*, compiled from a series of lectures given in southern Indian universities in 1928. It was obvious to him that no improvement could be expected from the *mullahs* or clerics, stuffed with obsolete notions and prejudices, especially in the villages. Two poems about them, Nos. 4 and 40, are distinctly anti-clerical, even satirical. No. 7 evens the balance by ridiculing the Hindu temple and its grotesque idols.

There is a strong note of what must look like unorthodoxy in other poems. In No. 46, a dialogue between Gabriel and his former companion Satan, it is the latter who can boast of stirring up men to think and act boldly. He has regrets for the past, but no wish to be back again in a heaven where nothing happens. (Hell is not mentioned.) No. 50, on the tomb of Napoleon, in Paris, is a paean of praise to the warrior heroes of the past: Alexander, Tamberlane, and champions of Islam. Each was granted a brief spell (an 'innings' we might call it) to display his courage and prowess, and then followed

'the long nights of the grave.'

These must, it seems, signify extinction: no heaven awaited them, whether they had been Muslims or not. If so, we are being given a bold example of religious 'reconstruction'. The Koranic paradise could not be called an edifying one; it was time to assume—as my guide Dr Nazir Ahmad Shah, and doubtless many others did—that its rewards were purely symbolic.

Iqbal's grand, truly revolutionary poems were illuminated by the fires of the Great War and the overthrow of tsarism. *Bal-e-Jibril* ('Gabriel's Wing'), the most powerful Urdu collection, did not appear in book form until 1936, a dozen years after its Urdu predecessor *Bang-i-Dara* ('The signal for a party of pilgrims to resume their journey'). No doubt during this long interval many or most of the poems had been recited publicly, or had appeared in magazines. But these were troubled years, both within the empire and internationally, and it is not hard to guess that Iqbal received some admonishments not to make more trouble.

His poem No. 41, declares that all land belongs to God, who lends it out to landlords on trust for those who toil on it and raise its harvests. Thomas Carlyle had said much the same. What the two thought had not made much visible difference to either England or India. Landlordism continued to rule the roost in both. But in Iqbal's time the big landowners were the chief props and bulwarks of British power. He went on writing politically, but in a more subdued key, or one more often directed against external targets, with a generalizing tendency to denounce the imperialistic 'West' and chide the supine 'East'.

Iqbal died shortly before my arrival in his historic city of Lahore. I had therefore no chance to meet him; a great pity for me—he was said to be very accessible and fond of discussion. But there were many others who had known him, and could talk about him. Hence arose these translations, composed in their first version at the Aitchison College of Lahore, where I was teaching during the War years. I am still in touch with a very few of my pupils from that time. I was also kept busy with talks and programmes about the War and its background, for the newly established All India Radio, which was left a good deal to its own devices. This work grew more pressing as the Japanese army drew closer to India, and public opinion grew more equivocal.

I was getting to know a variety of people, a good many of them active socialists, pro-British since 1941 because of the growing pro-Russia trend. A fondness for hearing poetry recited—rather than reading it—was surprisingly widespread. I can still see in my mind's eye a stalwart young Punjabi—a Hindu—declaiming with immense feeling the command to the angels (in my poem No. 39): 'Rise, and from their slumber wake the poor ones of my world!' In later years, I learned, he wrote songs for the blossoming Bombay cinema.

Iqbal was concerned first and foremost with the destinies of his own community; but fundamentally he seems concerned rather with Man, the human race, and this is what can be said to give his work a universal relevance. In an early poem (No. 16) he ascends into heaven and complains to the Almighty of the Italian invasion of Libya, then Turkish, in 1911. In a later, Persian poem No. 113, called 'Solitude' (every poet wrote one or two lyrics under this title), he speaks for all human beings, in their pitifully isolated condition. He roams through

the universe, only to be repulsed by the sea, a mountain, the moon—
the whole of Nature—, and finally confronts the Almighty again: he is
answered only with a smile.

Looking once more at my old copies of Iqbal, and tattered
dictionaries, has reminded me of many associates who gave me help
or encouragement. One I recall was Sufi Ghulam Mustafa, a teacher of
Persian at Government College. He pointed out to me on one occasion
the exquisitely undulating line about flower-colours in No. 28

Ude, ude, nile, nile, pile, pile, perhan.

Sufi Sahib, as he was known, had taken the pen-name of *Tabassum*, or
'Smile', well suited to his cheerful and hospitable disposition. I hope his
own poems are still known. In one he declared that his people would
never find happiness until they had

'Their own country, their own rule'
(*Apna desh aour apna raj*).

Iqbal's rejoinder to Goethe in No. 114, and the next poem as well
as several others, show his image of himself as one always dedicated
to further explorations. He often calls himself a *traveller*, never content
to sit still. This can be seen in Nos. 10, 30, 115, and the concluding
quatrain, a kind of epitaph. It is from Persian, and was chosen partly
because its last two lines lend themselves in English to a particular
rhythmic effect, but more because it compresses into so few words the
poet's restless sense of perpetual seeking, and loneliness, and
uncertainty as to how far he had come, and what, after all, his message
really had been. He was, it seems, something of a mystery to himself,
and dubious of the admirers who thought they understood him. His
perplexity has something in it reminiscent of that other poet,
Wordsworth, 'Moving about in worlds not realised'. Perhaps all true
artists have had some such sensation. Iqbal asked for the quatrain to
be inscribed on his tomb, which stands now in the great courtyard of
the Imperial Mosque.

I cannot take leave of Lahore without repeating my indebtendess to
my friend Dr Nazir Ahmad Shah. His help and advice to me were
invaluable and unfailing. I got to know him first when I was at
Cambridge, and he was wrestling with some obscure zoological riddle
at Imperial College, London. His path through life was not without

private troubles, but later on, as Principal of Government College, he earned unbounded respect from high and low. After retirement he edited some of the old folk-poems of the Punjab, very imaginative and too long neglected. His religion was free of animosity against any other; he was an embodiment of everything good in the culture of his people.

My (and Dr Nazir's) Sikh friend, Iqbal Singh, who died at Delhi a year or two ago, was too much an idealist to deserve his first name, whose central meaning is 'prosperity'. Instead he earned numberless friends, and a literary reputation. His early work on Buddhism was republished forty years later. His study of the poet Iqbal, *The Ardent Pilgrim*, came out in 1951, and was revised for a second edition, published by the Oxford University Press at Delhi, in 1997. An Urdu translation of it was done by the Oxford University Press at Karachi, in 2003. His admiring but judicious critique is a book not to be missed; though he points out that a good deal of further information about Iqbal and his life still remains to be gathered up.

Victor Kiernan,
Stow, Selkirkshire,
18 February 2003

PREFACE TO THE 1955 EDITION

Muhammad Iqbal, the 'Poet of the East,' lived a life outwardly of which there is little to be said, and inwardly of which little is known. Born at Sialkot in the province of Punjab in 1873, of a pious middle-class family, he was educated in both Indian and Western culture, and in 1899 graduated from the Government College at Lahore, the capital of the province. For six years he was a lecturer in philosophy at Lahore; from 1905 to 1908 he was in Europe, studying philosophy at Trinity College, Cambridge, and in Germany, and also qualifying in law. After two more years as a lecturer he resigned from the educational service of a Government of which he had become an outspoken critic. He continued to live in Lahore, earning enough as a lawyer to defray his very modest expenses, while devoting himself chiefly to his studies and to poetry. By 1922, when he (surprisingly) accepted a knighthood, he was recognized as the most eminent writer of Muslim India. During the next ten years he emerged, though never very wholeheartedly, into the public life of his province and of Muslim India, and he was a Muslim delegate to a Round Table Conference in London in 1931. On this occasion he also visited Spain, Italy, and some other countries. At home his mode of existence was remarkably stationary; he sat in his house reading, writing, and talking with a continual stream of callers to whom he was always accessible. Of his domestic life little seems to be recorded except that he was married three times. He died in 1938; seventy thousand people are said to have followed his funeral procession.

Though Iqbal's life was uneventful, his corner of the world and of history was a very complex one, and the intricacy of the forces that made him is reflected in his linguistic equipment. For his colloquial language he had the Punjabi speech common to the whole province; it has something of the flavour and character of very broad Scots. The language of his rulers, and the medium through which he was in contact with the modern world, was English (he knew also German): in English he wrote prose, notably *The Reconstruction of Religious Thought in Islam*. The written language of the Punjab, and the spoken as well as written language of some other (chiefly Muslim) regions, was Urdu: a blending brought about since medieval times by contact between Hindu India and Persian-speaking invaders and settlers. In basic syntax and vocabulary it is identical with Hindi; but its script is Arabic instead of Sanskrit, and its learned vocabulary Persian and Arabic instead of Sanskrit. Iqbal's 'classical' language was Persian: not the modern vernacular of Iran, but the older form brought into India in past centuries. His religious language, finally, in which he was well versed, was Arabic.

Apart from a handful of Persian poems the verse chosen here for translation is taken from Iqbal's work in Urdu, which consists of short and medium-length pieces only. The selection extends over the whole of his working life, and may serve to illustrate its main phases; it includes a good proportion of those poems that have been most admired by the judicious. Although up to 1908 Iqbal composed chiefly in Urdu, he did not publish his first Urdu collection, *Bāng-i-Darā*, until 1924; this ranges therefore from juvenile verse to his fully developed style, as in the *Khizar-i-Rāh* group of poems (No. 18 in this translation) written in 1922. *Bāl-i-Jibrīl*, published in 1935, is his acknowledged masterpiece in Urdu; it was followed in 1936 by *Zarb-i-Kalīm*, a collection mostly of short epigrams, critical rather than lyrical though often highly polished. *Armaghān-i-Hejāz* appeared posthumously in 1938 and contained his latest work in both Urdu and Persian.

In Urdu, Iqbal is allowed to have been far the greatest poet of this century, and by most critics to be the only equal of Ghalib (1797-1869). He was the first prominent Urdu poet who was a native of the Punjab, and his emergence marked a shift of Muslim Indian culture away from the Deccan and the United Provinces towards the north. In Persian, in which he published six volumes of mainly long poems between 1915 and 1936, his rank is less easy to determine. He was very exceptional among Urdu writers of this century in reviving the older habit of writing in Persian; he did so partly, it is said, because he found Persian better suited to the philosophical subjects he wanted to write on, and partly in order to reach a wider audience, Persian being the literary *lingua franca* of a large part of the Muslim world. One may wonder whether he gained more readers outside India by this means than he lost at home. At any rate, his Persian volumes are more or less complete works on philosophical themes, with the exception of *Pyām-i-Mashriq* (1923) and *Zabūr-i-ÔAjam*(1927): much of these two consists of short lyrical pieces, considered by the judicious to represent, poetically, the best of his work in Persian. By comparison the Urdu poems, addressed to a real and familiar audience close at hand, have the merit of being direct, spontaneous utterances on tangible subjects; and it is probably the case that nearly all the leading ideas of the 'serious' Persian works are expressed more briefly, sometimes more effectively, in the Urdu.

Iqbal might be summed up as, in the broadest sense, a *political* poet, one concerned with men as social beings. Art, he said, has for duty the strengthening of mankind in face of its problems; and he would have agreed with Wordsworth in desiring to be regarded as a teacher, or as nothing. In his experimental years he was under the influence of English romanticism and nature-poetry, not always of the best models (he even wrote adaptations of Longfellow). He was also working in the well-beaten track of Persian-Indian literature, with its ogling lovers and other such trifling and artificial themes, and its stock of imagery and symbolism derived in large part from the winecup and wineshop and garden of the old Sufi mystics or pseudo-mystics. But quite soon Iqbal was pushing his way towards more solid ground; and it was because he grappled with the great questions of his world that he has a place in the history of twentieth-century Asia. He was helped by the fact that in his society poetry, like religion, was still a living thing, and could be made a living force. It came naturally to Iqbal to write verses in which God or Satan spoke about the Poet of the East. The great popularity of the *mushāʿara*, the symposium in which poets recite or chant their verses, is an illustration of this. Iqbal's verses were not limited to circulation through the printing-press, and they could and did reach wide circles even of the illiterate. He was helped also by the common stock of literary tropes and allusions whose use in their old character he soon outgrew. The vocabulary of the wineshop, or of the Persian garden with its roses, breezes, nightingales, moths, candles, could be used—is still being used today, even by some writers of ultra-modern opinions—as a medium for the discussion of new problems. Old phrases with new significances provided a continuity, a harmonizing element, lacking to Western poets who have tried to discuss a hard, crude contemporary world in the bare language of today.

The situation from which Iqbal contemplated the world was that of the middle classes of Muslim India, in process of separating themselves off from the feudal order of landlords and peasants, and leading a general revival of the Muslim community in India. Once the reigning power in India, and after the Mughal collapse, the British conquest, and the failure of the Mutiny pushed into the background, the Muslims had for long remained baffled and resentful. Meanwhile the Hindus, whose commercial habits made it easier for them to acclimatize themselves to the new conditions, were going ahead. After Sir Syed Ahmad Khan (d. 1898) and the 'Aligarh movement' had summoned the Muslims to get to grips with the new age, it was natural that the Muslim middle classes should come to be drawn in behind the Hindu nationalist movement led by the Indian National Congress. Iqbal's early poetry held up the ideal of a united and free India, with Muslims and Hindus living side by side like brothers. In the Punjab, where they were in roughly equal numbers, and much intermingled, such an ideal had a special urgency.

This was not to last long. Finding its more immediate and palpable obstacle in the superior Hindu wealth and organization, rather than in British rule, the Muslim middle classes, despite various fluctuations, were to turn away from the Indian National Congress in the direction charted by the Muslim League. So far as Iqbal was concerned, his first period ended with his stay in Europe from 1905 to 1908. There he absorbed new ideas, and was influenced by several thinkers, notably Hegel, Bergson, and above all Nietzsche. He took from them what was congenial to his own needs as a member of a community growing conscious of its own backwardness—the sense of evolution and history, of advance through effort and struggle. This was to lay the basis for the chief formal doctrine associated with his name, that of _Khudī_, or 'Selfhood': the dynamic individual personality developed through practical activity in the world, as against the lingering Sufi ideal of passive contemplation and mystic absorption. With such ideas Iqbal was clothing Individualism in one more of those innumerable costumes in which it has been travelling the world since the decay of the old feudal order in Europe. But the Muslim middle class was too weak, and history had gone too far by now, with individualism already challenged by socialism, for him to fall in love with any mere _laissez-faire_ self-assertiveness. Soon after his first long poem, in praise of _Self_ (1915), came another in praise of _Selflessness_.[1] What he was really concerned with was the healthy development of the individual within a healthy community.

---

[1] See _The Mysteries of Selflessness_, trans. Professor A.J. Arberry ('Wisdom of the East Series', John Murray, 1953).

Such a community he no longer expected to find in a united India; but he was equally far from seeking it in any imitation of Western nationalism, that counterpart, at the other pole of morbid excess, to Western individualism. Soon after his return to India he was deeply stirred by events like the Italian attack on Turkey and seizure of Tripoli in 1911. Then his already deeply undermined respect for the boasted civilization of the white men was blown to pieces by the Great War. From that time on he held up his mirror to Europe's face in the spirit of Hamlet confronting his mother. He would, I think, have wished his poems to be translated into English; at the end he was even thinking of writing in English verse himself.

While the Muslims of India moved towards the Muslim League, Iqbal's ideals shifted towards Islam. In Sir Syed Ahmad's time the appeal of Muslim reawakening had been somewhat negative: it had been mainly a question of clearing away conservative prejudice and setting the Muslims free to go in for modern education and pursuits. Gradually, for instance in the hands of the poet Ḥālī about the end of the nineteenth century, it assumed a more positive form. Iqbal was coming to the conclusion that the business of the Muslims was not to open their ears to the teachings of others, since this modern world had no message of life to give them; but to open their minds and souls to the message of their own faith, their own past, their own genius as a community. Earlier work must be continued, of clearing away the rubbish of lifeless scholasticism, corruption, superstition: also, Islam should be conceived as a philosophy and a mode of life still evolving and expanding. Fundamentally, however, its principles were fixed and eternal. Only Islam, he was to argue from now on, could reconcile individual and community, tradition and progress, reason and faith, Church and State. In practice, his wrestlings with these intransigent opposites never succeeded in reconciling them very thoroughly. They were nourished by underlying contradictions in a movement that was trying simultaneously to return to the past and to discover the future, to worship changelessness and change. For a community situated as the Indian Muslims were, it was only possible to regain consciousness of life and confidence in life by turning back to the past; on the other hand, it was perilously easy for the real or fancied glories of the past to become substitutes for serious thinking or rational decision.

Muslims, as compared with Hindus, gained in one way but lost in another by the fact that their religion was much simpler and more coherent, and more readily seemed to offer solutions for problems of modern society. Generally speaking, in India in recent decades the average educated young Muslim has been religious, the Hindu sceptical.

Iqbal might convince himself that he had the master-key in his hands, yet the doors seemed to remain obstinately shut on him. At the end of his life the true, inward, essential revival of Islamic virtue, whose prophet he had made himself, seemed to him to lie as far away as at the beginning. Reason and faith had not fused after all, and it may have been an uneasy sensation of this that made him at times somewhat querulously critical of the West, as the worshipper of mind to the exclusion of soul. When he thought most clearly and wrote most finely—the two usually went together—he was well aware that the true antithesis of his age was not between East and West, but between more fundamental things. These he expressed in a variety of ways: the history of the twentieth century is writing them down as the principles of social justice and of social injustice. What made Iqbal a great poet was his hatred of injustice. It also at times made him fall into that undiscriminating aversion from Europe (as well as from Hinduism, in another way) which has been the worst of all Europe's gifts, good and bad, to other lands. Seeing the League of Nations, or capitalist democracy, as shams—primarily because neither had any interest in justice for colonial peoples—he refused to see genuine ideals struggling towards the light in them. He could be misled, like a great many Indians, into a certain approval of fascism because it seemed to contradict those impostures, and because Germany and Italy were anti-British; though Iqbal's instinct was sound, and the fate of Abyssinia soon freed him from any illusions about Mussolini and his like. Similarly, revulsion against Western misuse of science could make Iqbal sound as if he was condemning science and even reason itself, and exalting passion and instinct and intuition blindly. To jump in this way out of the European frying-pan was only to fall into an equally European fire.

At home in the Punjab Iqbal's mind went on growing and developing—his great period was roughly 1920-35, remarkably late in a poet's life—, holding on to life in spite of the shockingly parochial atmosphere of Lahore, and the politically very backward conditions of a province dominated by feudal landlords and foreign policemen.

Neither Muslim League nor Indian National Congress had much organized strength here, and the political vacuum at least allowed Iqbal's ideas to remain flexible, if at times incalculable. It is to be noted that the Punjab was comparatively prosperous, its peasantry much less deeply pauperized than those of other provinces. The peasant had not lost his old self-respect as an individual, nor found a new self-respect as a member of a movement; which helps to account both for the migration of Urdu poetry to the Punjab and for the political torpor that made the Punjabi a byword in India. Iqbal's community was still in a semi-feudal, pre-industrial stage, while exposed to all the currents of a more modern environment. Such a social context is not uncongenial to poetry. Iqbal, a man of the middle class, was close enough both to the landlords and princes above it, and to the labourers and peasants below it, to be able to look at life through the eyes of all of them, and his ideal of religious brotherhood derived from this fact. Islam offered the intellectual a link with his fellow-men of all ranks, and seemed to offer a means of preventing them from breaking apart from one another, as they were beginning to do under the impact of new forces. Such an outlook was more favourable to poetic inspiration than any limited viewpoint of a single section of society, high or low, would have been. The French Revolution, which carried into effect the aspirations of an industrial bourgeoisie, wrote no poetry about the business. Much the same is true of the Russian Revolution and the aspirations of an industrial proletariat. Iqbal, like Shakespeare or Goethe in other modes and degrees, belonged to a stage in which society had begun but not yet finished crystallizing into exclusive sections, and emotion had not yet fully crystallized into thought.

Iqbal hated injustice; his protest, first made in the name of India, continued in the name of Islam; in this form it was reinforced, rather than superseded, by a protest in the name of the common man, the disinherited of all lands.

Pan-Islamic thinking had already appeared in nineteenth-century India. Iqbal, as usual, put new wine into old bottles, not always very well suited to it. His interest in the now fermenting Near and Middle East was fresh and vital, because he was himself a part of a great historical process, the 'revolt of Asia'. Sympathizing with small nations under the domination of the predatory empires, he dreamed of a liberated world of Islam in the form of a kind of federation linked by common faith and ideals. Any such vision was bound to run into practical difficulties. The Indian Muslim has got into the habit of anxiously concerning himself about the fate of Muslims abroad who have taken exceedingly little interest in *his* fate. Iqbal, like so many others during the *Khilāfat* agitation at the end of the Great War, entangled himself in sympathy for Turkey as the enemy of the West, forgetting that Turkish imperialism was as bad as Western imperialism for the Arabs. Then, for a Muslim country like Reza Shah's Iran to go in for progress on 'modern' lines was in Iqbal's view a dereliction of Islamic duty; but it was equally bad for countries like Afghanistan to make no progress at all. Seeing no other way of reconciling religion and progress, sceptical of parliamentary methods, and carried away by recollections of departed heroes of Islam, he was always scanning the horizon for Great Men who were to descend from the skies and lead their propels into promised lands. Inevitably he was often disillusioned. Asia's Mussolinis were not, after all, much different from Europe's.

Iqbal felt for poor men as he felt for poor nations, and as he grew to maturity and Asia experienced the impact of the Russian and Chinese revolutions, the social problem came more and more to the front of his mind. There was little of a socialist movement, because there was little industry, in the Punjab; but in the first and purest age of Islam that Iqbal was looking back to, as in primitive Christianity, there was much that could be equated with the modern spirit of reform, and he always stressed its elements of fraternity and social justice. Certainly he went much further in his desire for social reform than the politicians of the Muslim League ever did. It has been noticed as one of the many paradoxes in Iqbal that he was almost alone among Urdu poets in moving towards the Muslim League, which had no 'social programme', and yet it was also he who inducted the theme of the workman and his sufferings into Urdu poetry. Whether he could at any time be properly called a 'socialist' has been debated. Socialism in its systematic detail remained on the whole outside his purview; it may be fair to add that the nearest successors to this poet who left no literary disciples are the Urdu socialist poets of to-day. Iqbal knew, if he did not always remember, that Utopia lay in the future, not in the past, and that it was to be won by human effort, not by incantations. But what kind of effort? By the time he was writing *Bāl-i-Jibrīl*, even if he still thought of socialism as too materialistic by itself, he thought well enough of Lenin to bring him into Heaven, where however he only allowed Lenin to utter a passionate denunciation of imperialism and capitalism and call upon *God* to destroy them. In his last important Urdu poem—*Satan's Parliament*, written in 1936—Iqbal made his last approach to the problem. He imagined Satan's counsellors anxiously debating the spread of Karl Marx's message through the world, as subversive of the reign of evil. Then he turned back to his former thinking. Marxism, Satan admits, may indeed be deplorable, but what he really fears as the danger to his power on earth is a revival of Islam, and in particular of the true Islamic teaching on wealth and poverty—the Quranic principle that *The earth is God's*, and that possession of property is only trusteeship: this is the real, the grand 'revolution'. Iqbal wanted to abolish the ill-treatment of peasant by landlord, without abolishing landlordism. A revolution consisting of four Arabic words may have the merit of being quiet and inoffensive; whether it will do any good to a peasant remains for demonstration. India and China have since then been attacking the agrarian problem along other lines.

Beyond this point Iqbal could not go; it was the end of his pilgrimage. He had ended by being, in some ways, the prisoner of the ideas that had promised to liberate him. All his life as a poet he had been using the hard, distinct, unyielding thoughts of a bygone age as supports round which the softer tendrils growing out of the amorphous sensations of his own age could twine themselves and climb. Dante and Milton did the same. The typical *good* Western poetry of the past hundred years has not been tempted to do so, because it has been negative and unconstructive, content to appeal to corners and fractions of disintegrated minds. The poets of affirmation have always incurred artistic risks, such as the mass of scholastic rubbish that clogs the wings of Dante's angels; more grave has been the danger that their work would rather help the past to survive than the future to be born. It remains the task of writers of our epoch to show whether poetry both imaginative and profitable to mankind can be reared on a framework of ideas genuinely contemporary and still growing.

In 1930, Iqbal had spoken to the Muslim League at its Allahabad session in favour of the then almost unheard-of idea of a separate State for the Muslims in north-west India. No doubt he had in mind the introduction of pure Islamic principles, including those of social reform: it would be a kind of flight from the fleshpots of Egypt to the wilderness of the ideal. He had always condemned the nationalism of the West as founded on mere animal ties of blood instead of on harmony of ideals. The nationalism of India was developing, before his death, tendencies still more irrational and morbid; in the Punjab suspicion, fear and greed helped to deepen the gulf between the religious communities. Iqbal had been fond of calling on Providence to set before his people once more the old wine they had drunk in their great days. For throwing poison in the cup, many must share the blame; obstinate politicians on both sides, foreigners playing the game of divide and rule, and in some measure Iqbal himself. He had talked of the importance of a peaceful understanding between Muslims and Hindus; he had also, in his time, indulged in unguarded rhetoric about holy wars and the sword of Islam, and extolled *action* as if it were an end in itself. Doubtless many other on both sides said the same things, but few with his authority and none with his eloquence. The holy war he would have seen if he had lived another decade, and most certainly would have recoiled from in horror, was the gigantic massacre of 1947, one of the most frightful catastrophes of even the twentieth century, in which the Muslims and Hindus of the Punjab perished by hundreds of thousands. Years before, thinking of the Great War, he had written: 'That is not the rosy dawn of a new age on the horizon of the West, but a torrent of blood.' The same might have been written now of his own horizon of the East.

In the new State that now had to find its place in the world, Iqbal was canonized as a founding father and hoisted on to an official pedestal. That dead poets should moulder in government shrines while living poets moulder in government jails is a not unfamiliar irony of history. A contest between obscurantism and enlightenment was inevitable; and on certain of the issues that became controversial, such as that of *purdah*, Iqbal's opinion could be cited by the unprogressive. Nevertheless, it is permissible to hope that the leaven he left in men's minds is working more potently on the other side. A poet's influence is Protean. Among those numerous Muslims and Hindus who in the nightmare days of 1947 saved the lives of members of the other community at the risk of their own, I know of some, and there must have been many, who had breathed Iqbal's verses with their native air. It was, after all, his lifelong teaching that the spirit is more than the letter, that religion must always be on its guard against the Pharisee, the dogmatist, and the charlatan, and that a people must go forward or die.

The following works may be further consulted:

T.G. Bailey, *Urdu Literature* (Calcutta and London, 1932).
Mohammed Sadiq, *Twentieth-Century Urdu Literature* (Baroda, 1947).

Sardar Jafri, 'Urdu and Hindi' (a valuable article in *Indian Literature*, Bombay, 1953, no. 1).

W.C. Smith, *Modern Islam in India* (London, 1946).

K.G. Saiyidain, *Iqbal's Educational Philosophy* (Lahore, 1938).

Abdulla Anwar Beg, *The Poet of the East* (Lahore, 1939).

Syed Abdul Vahid, *Iqbal, His Art and Thought* (Lahore, 1944). and— incomparably the best study known to me of Iqbal—Iqbal Singh, *The Ardent Pilgrim* (London, 1951).

NOTE ON THE TRANSLATIONS

In translating these poems I have tried first of all to give the sense of the originals as exactly as possible, without addition or subtraction. As regards form, I have kept to regular metres throughout. Iqbal was strictly classical in his versification, and the more experimental style of the moderns, in colloquial diction, unrhymed verse, and irregular metre, owes nothing to him. Even 'free verse' in very modern Urdu, it may be remarked, is only licentious enough to admit lines containing uneven numbers of the same regular feet (as in the English of no. 9 below).

Iqbal's normal unit is the self-contained couplet of two lines or hemistichs (*miṣra'a*) of equal length. At times he arranges lines in groups of three (as in 90) or, more often, five (111). Generally the number of lines in the translation is the same as in the original. Occasionally each Urdu line has been turned into two English lines (e.g. 66, 92, 113); in no. 13 each English line represents two of Urdu. In a poem like no. 104, whose length and manner make blank verse the only choice, and where the Urdu lines are longer, there is no close correspondence in the number of lines. Rhyme I have sometimes omitted and often rearranged or simplified. Rhyming is much easier, and as a result less emphatic, in Urdu than in English. One form of poem, the _ghazal_, plays so big a part in Urdu that I have reproduced its rhyme-scheme (AABACADA...) in a group of seventeen poems from the first part of *Bāl-i-Jibrīl*; including in some of them (the 1st, 3rd, 4th and 9th of this group) a *radīf*, a word or words recurring after each rhyming syllable.

Urdu metres, mainly derived from Persian, are varied and effective. They are based on a quantitative system which divides the foot into sound-units composed of long vowels and vowelized or unvowelized consonants. Urdu has, properly, no accent; on the other hand, Urdu verse, evolved for public declamation, can be recited with a very strong accentual rhythm, the stresses falling on almost any syllable in accordance with the quantitative pattern. This pattern cannot be reproduced with much fidelity in English, where quantity plays a considerable but an undefined and unsystematic part, and where two 'long' (or 'strong') syllables cannot be made to stand side by side in a fixed order, as they do habitually in Urdu verse.

Iqbal's predilection is for long, grave, slow-moving lines; it would be monotonous and heavy to employ such a proportion of long lines in English. Some of his commonest forms may be roughly expressed as:

(a)　　| – ˘ – – | – ˘ – – | – ˘ – – | – ˘ – |

with a stress on either the first or the third syllable of each foot;

(b)　　| ˘ — — – | ˘ — — – | ˘ — — – | ˘ – |

(c)　　| –́ – ˘ | –́ – ˘ | –́ – ˘ | –́ |

Examples of modes of approximation to *(a)* are 18 (2) and 18 (4) ; and to *(b)*, 1 and 2. In 39 can be seen how *(c)* tends to become in English (with the final syllable dropped):

| –́ ˘ ˘̄ ˘ | –́ ˘ ˘̄ ˘ | –́ ˘ ˘̄ ˘ | –́ |

Among shorter lines, there is a resemblance of a sort between;

| ˘ –́ — | ˘ –́ — | ˘ –́ — |

and the ordinary English line of five iambic feet (e.g. 36 (1), 53); and the line used in 7 is fairly close to the original, where, however, all the endings are 'feminine'. In metres in what may be called 'triple time', Iqbal's most characteristic rhythm, employed for instance in the originals of 32, 44, 49, is:

| ˘ –́ – | ˘ –́ – | ˘ –́ – | ˘ –́ (–) |

—which becomes in English (e.g. 49) merely anapaestic and comparatively frivolous.

In a few cases, where Iqbal's metre seems to have some unusual charm or novelty, I have tried to transpose it into English. In 27 it is:

| – ˘ ˘ – | ˘ – ˘ – ‖ – ˘ ˘ – | ˘ – ˘ – |

and in 30:

$$|- \cup|\underline{/}\|- \cup|\underline{/}|$$

In these two *ghazals* the English lines are printed with a break, to
make the caesura more distinct. In 37 the original resembles the
pentameter of an elegiac couplet:

$$|- \cup \cup|- \cup \cup|-\|- \cup \cup|- \cup \cup|-|$$

I have allowed spondees here for dactyls by way of variety, and have
omitted the complex rhyme-scheme, which includes many internal
rhymes. In 45 I have omitted the final syllable of the original, which
consists of four feet in the measure:

$$| \cup - \cup \underline{/} \underline{\ }|$$ (The rhyme-scheme of the original is the same as that of
the *ghazal*.) In 114 the rhythm:

$$| \cup \cup \underline{/}| \cup \check{\ } \cup| - \cup\| \cup \cup \underline{/}| \cup \check{\ } \cup|- \cup|$$

sounds more light and airy than in English. Otherwise I have chosen
metres because they seemed to fit the English words or to offer some
kind of analogy to the sound of the original. In Part IV I have tried the
effect of a few classical metres.

In this new edition which differs from that published in India several
years ago, I have omitted a number of poems of lesser interest,
especially from Iqbal's earlier period, and have added those that now
make up Parts IV and V. All the others I have revised considerably,
and I hope improved.

It would have been far beyond my competence to translate these
poems without a great deal of help from experts, and I am grateful for
the very generous help of a number of scholars whom I had the
privilege of knowing in the Punjab, and some of whom had had the
privilege of knowing Iqbal. Among them I must thank most warmly of
all my friend Dr Nazir Ahmad Shah. His guidance and instruction
have always been indefatigably patient, and his knowledge and taste I
rely on implicitly. I am also deeply indebted to three leading scholars
of Lahore: Sufi Ghulam Mustafa *Tabassum*, Khwaja Abd-ul-Hamid,
and the late Dr M.D. Taseer. Two former colleagues of mine, Mr
Anwar Sikandar Khan and Mr M.A. Siddiqi, gave me valuable

assistance, and Mr D.A. Daoud, an Egyptian archaeologist, has helped me more recently to decipher some of those Arabic plurals that are the real curse of the Middle East. In undertaking this revised edition I have been encouraged by the sympathetic interest and criticism of Mr A.S. Bokhari, MrG.A. Shepperson, Dr E.J. Hobsbawm, and Mr J.L. Cranmer-Byng.

Of Iqbal's other work his Urdu poems *Shikwah and Jawāb-i-Shikwah* (from *Bāng-i-Darā*) have been translated into English verse, as *Complaint and Answer*, by Altaf Husain (Lahore, 1943). Of his Persian poetry, *Secrets of the Self* (*Asrār-i-Khudī*) was translated in 1920 by Professor R.A. Nicholson; *The Tulip of Sinai* (a series of quatrains from *Pyām-i-Mashriq*) by Professor A.J. Arberry in 1947; and *The Mysteries of Selflessness* (*Rumūz-i-Bēkhudī*) by the same scholar in 1953, in the 'Wisdom of the East' series—a series referred to by Iqbal himself in a note in *Bāl-i-Jibrīl*, p. 137.

PART I

BANG-I-DARA

THE CALL OF THE ROAD

1. A Withered Rose

How shall I call you now a flower—
    Tell me, oh withered rose!
How call you that beloved for whom
    The nightingale's heart glows?
The winds' soft ripples cradled you
    And rocked your bygone hours,
And your name once was Laughing Rose
    In the country of flowers;
With the dawn breezes that received
    Your favours you once played,
Like a perfumer's vase your breath
    Sweetened the garden glade.

These eyes are full, and drops like dew
    Fall thick on you again;
This desolate heart finds dimly its
    Own image in your pain,
A record drawn in miniature
    Of all its sorry gleaning:
My life was all a life of dreams,
    And you—you are its meaning.
I tell my stories as the reed
    Plucked from its native wild
Murmurs; oh Rose, listen! I tell
    The grief of hearts exiled.

گُلِ پژمُردہ

کس زباں سے اے گُلِ پژمُردہ تجھ کو گُل کہوں ۔۔۔ کس طرح تجھ کو تمنائے دلِ بُلبل کہوں

تھی کبھی موجِ صبا گہوارۂ جُنباں ترا ۔۔۔ نام تھا صحنِ گُلستاں میں گُلِ خنداں ترا

تیرے احساں کا نسیم صبح کو اقرار تھا

باغ تیرے دم سے گویا طبلۂ عطّار تھا

تجھ پہ برساتا ہے شبنم دیدۂ گریاں مرا ۔۔۔ ہے نہاں تیری اُداسی میں دل ویراں مرا

میری بربادی کی ہے چھوٹی سی اک تصویر تُو ۔۔۔ خواب میری زندگی تھی جس کی ہے تعبیر تُو

ہمچونے از نیستانِ خود حکایت می کنم ۔۔۔ بشنو اے گُل! از جُدائیہا شکایت می کنم

2. New Moon

THE day's bright launch has foundered in the whirlpool of the
    Nile,
On the river's face one fragment floats eddyingly awhile;
Into the bowl of heaven the twilight's crimson blood-drops run—
Has Nature with her lancet pricked the hot veins of the sun?
—Is that an earring, that the sky has thieved from Evening's
    bride,
Or through the water does some silvery fish, quivering, glide?

Your caravan holds on its way, though no trumpet be blown;
Your voice still murmurs, though no mortal ear may catch its
    tone.
All shapes of life that wanes or grows before us you display:
Where is your native land? towards what country lies your
    way?
You who still wander yet still keep your path, take me with
    you,
Take me now while these throbbing thorns of torment pierce
me through!
I grope for light, I anguish in this earth-abode, a child
In the schoolroom of existence, like pale mercury quick and
    wild.

ماہِ نَو

ایک ٹکڑا تیرا پھرتا ہے روئے آبِ نیل	ٹوٹ کر خورشید کی کشتی ہوئی غرقابِ نیل
نشترِ قدرت نے کیا کھولی ہے فصدِ آفتاب؟	طشتِ گردوں میں ٹپکتا ہے شفق کا خونِ ناب

چرخ نے بالی چرالی ہے عروسِ شام کی؟

نیل کے پانی میں یا مچھلی ہے سیم خام کی؟

گوشِ انساں سن نہیں سکتا تری آوازِ پا	قافلہ تیرا رواں بے منتِ بانگِ درا
ہے وطن تیرا کدھر؟ کس دیس کو جاتا ہے تُو؟	گھٹنے بڑھنے کا سماں آنکھوں کو دکھلاتا ہے تُو
خارِ حسرت کی خلش رکھتی ہے اب بیکل مجھے	ساتھ اے سیارۂ ثابت نما لے چل مجھے

نور کا طالب ہوں، گھبراتا ہوں اس بستی میں مَیں

طفلکِ سیماب پا ہوں مکتبِ ہستی میں مَیں

3. *Man and Nature*

WATCHING at daybreak the bright sun come forth
I asked the assembled host of heaven and earth—

Your radiant looks are kindled by that glowing orb's warm
    beams
        That turn to rippling silver your flowing streams;

That sun it is that clothes you in these ornaments of light,
        And whose torch burns to keep your concourse bright.
Your roses and rose-gardens are pictures of Paradise
        Where the scripture of *The Sun* paints its device;
Scarlet the mantle of the flower, and emerald of the tree,
        Green and red sylphs of your consistory;
Your tall pavilion, the blue sky, is fringed with tasselled gold
        When round the horizon ruddy clouds are rolled,
And when into evening's goblet your rose-tinted nectar
        flows
            How lovely the twilight's soft vermilion glows!
Your station is exalted, and your splendour : over all
        Your creatures light lies thick, a dazzling pall;
To your magnificence the dawn is one high hymn of praise,
        No rag of night lurks on in that sun's blaze.
And I—I too inhabit this abode of light; but why
        Is the star burned out that rules *my* destiny?
Why chained in the dark, past reach of any ray,
        Ill-faring and ill-fated and ill-doing must I stay?

اِنسان اور بزمِ قدرت

صبح خورشیدِ دَرخشاں کو جو دیکھا میں نے
پرتوِ مہر کے دم سے ہے اُجالا تیرا
مہر نے نور کا زیور تجھے پہنایا ہے
گُل و گلزار ترے خُلد کی تصویریں ہیں
سرخ پوشاک ہے پھولوں کی، درختوں کی ہری
ہے ترے خیمۂ گردوں کی طلائی جھالر
کیا بھلی لگتی ہے آنکھوں کو شفق کی لالی
رُتبہ تیرا ہے بڑا، شان بڑی ہے تیری
صبح اک گیت سراپا ہے تری سطوت کا
میں بھی آباد ہوں اس نور کی بستی میں مگر

بزمِ معمورۂ ہستی سے یہ پوچھا میں نے
سیم سیال ہے پانی ترے دریاؤں کا
تیری محفل کو اسی شمع نے چمکایا ہے
یہ سبھی سورۂ والشّمس کی تفسیریں ہیں
تیری محفل میں کوئی سبز، کوئی لال پری
بدلیاں لال سی آتی ہیں اُفق پر جو نظر
مئے گلرنگ خم شام میں تو نے ڈالی
پردۂ نور میں مَستور ہے ہر شے تیری
زیرِ خورشید نشاں تک بھی نہیں ظلمت کا
جل گیا پھر مری تقدیر کا اختر کیوں کر؟

نور سے دُور ہوں ظلمت میں گرفتار ہوں میں
کیوں سیہ روز، سیہ بخت، سیہ کار ہوں میں؟

  Speaking, I heard a voice from somewhere sound,
  From heaven's balcony or near the ground—
You are creation's gardener, flowers live only in your seeing,
  By your light hangs my being or not-being;
All beauty is in you : I am the tapestry of your soul;
  I am its key, but you are Love's own scroll.
The load that would not leave me you have lifted from my
  shoulder,
  You are all my chaotic work's re-moulder.
If I exist, it is only as a pensioner of the sun,
  Needing no aid from whom your spark burns on;
My gardens would turn wildernesses if the sun should fail,
  This sojourn of delight a prison's pale.
Oh you entangled in the snare of longing and unrest,
  Still ignorant of a thing so manifest—
Dullard, who should be proud, and still by self-contempt
  enslaved
  Bear in your brain illusion deep-engraved—
  If you would weigh your worth at its true rate,
No longer would ill-faring or ill-doing be your fate!

میں یہ کہتا تھا کہ آواز کہیں سے آئی   بامِ گردوں سے و یا صحنِ زمیں سے آئی

ہے ترے نور سے وابستہ مری بود و نمود   باغباں ہے تری ہستی پئے گلزارِ وجود

انجمن حُسن کی ہے تو، تری تصویر ہوں میں   عشق کا تو ہے صحیفہ، تری تفسیر ہوں میں

میرے بگڑے ہوئے کاموں کو بنایا تو نے   بار جو مجھ سے نہ اُٹھا، وہ اُٹھایا تو نے

نورِ خورشید کی محتاج ہے ہستی میری   اور بے منتِ خورشید چمک ہے تیری

ہو نہ خورشید تو ویراں ہو گلستاں میرا   منزلِ عیش کی جا، نام ہو زنداں میرا

آہ! اے رازِ عیاں کے نہ سمجھنے والے!   حلقۂ دامِ تمنا میں اُلجھنے والے!

ہائے غفلت! کہ تری آنکھ ہے پابندِ مجاز   ناز زیبا تھا تجھے، تو ہے مگر گرمِ نیاز

تو اگر اپنی حقیقت سے خبردار رہے

نہ سیہ روز رہے پھر، نہ سیہ کار رہے

4. *Virtue and Vice*

A MULLAH (I tell you his tale not a bit
With any ambition of airing my wit)
By ascetic deportment had won high repute,
In his praise neither gentle nor simple were mute.
God's will, he would say, just as meaning is latent
In words, through pure doctrine alone becomes patent.
His heart a full bowl : wine of piety worked there,
Though some dregs of conceit of omniscience lurked there—
He was wont to recount his own miracles, knowing
How this kept his tally of followers growing.
He had long been residing not far from my street,
So sinner and saint were accustomed to meet:
'This Iqbal', he once asked an acquaintance of mine,
'Is the dove of the tree in the literary line,
But how do religion's stern monishments seem
To agree with this man who at verse beats Kalim?
He thinks a Hindu not a heathen, I'm told,
A most casuistical notion to hold,
And some taints of the Shias' vile heresy sully
His mind—I have heard him extolling their Ali;
He finds room in our worship for music—which must
Be intended to level true faith with the dust!
As with poets so often, no scruple of duty
Deters him from meeting the vendors-of-beauty;
In the morning, devotions—at evening, the fiddle—
I have never been able to fathom this riddle.
Yet dawn, my disciples assure me, is not
More unsoiled than that youth is by blemish or spot;

زُہد اور رندی

اک مولوی صاحب کی سناتا ہوں کہانی
تیزی نہیں منظور طبیعت کی دکھانی

شہرہ تھا بہت آپ کی صوفی منشی کا
کرتے تھے ادب اُن کی اعالی و ادانی

کہتے تھے کہ پنہاں ہے تصوف میں شریعت
جس طرح کہ الفاظ میں مضمر ہوں معانی

لبریز مئے زُہد سے تھی دل کی صراحی
تھی نہ میں کہیں دردِ خیالِ ہمہ دانی

کرتے تھے بیاں آپ کرامات کا اپنی
منظور تھی تعداد مریدوں کی بڑھانی

مدت سے رہا کرتے تھے ہمسائے میں میرے
تھی رند سے زاہد کی ملاقات پرانی

حضرت نے مرے ایک شناسا سے یہ پوچھا
اقبالؔ، کہ ہے قُمرئ شمشادِ معانی

پابندیٔ احکامِ شریعت میں ہے کیسا؟
گو شعر میں ہے رشکِ کلیم ہمدانی

سنتا ہوں کہ کافر نہیں ہندو کو سمجھتا
ہے ایسا عقیدہ اثرِ فلسفہ دانی

ہے اس کی طبیعت میں تشیّع بھی ذرا سا
تفضیلِ علیؑ ہم نے سنی اس کی زبانی

سمجھا ہے کہ ہے راگ عبادات میں داخل
مقصود ہے مذہب کی مگر خاک اڑانی

کچھ عار اسے حُسن فروشوں سے نہیں ہے
عادت یہ ہمارے شعراء کی ہے پرانی

گانا جو ہے شب کو تو سحر کو ہے تلاوت
اس رمز کے اب تک نہ کھلے ہم پہ معانی

لیکن یہ سنا اپنے مریدوں سے ہے میں نے
بے داغ ہے مانند سحر اس کی جوانی

No Iqbal, but a heterogeneous creature,
His mind crammed with learning, with impulse his nature,
Familiar with vice, and with Holy Writ more
In divinity, doubtless, as deep as Mansur;
What the fellow is really, I cannot make out—
Is it founding some brand-new Islam he's about?'
—Thus the great man protracted his reverend chatter,
And in short made a very long tale of the matter.
In our town, all the world hears of every transaction:
I soon got reports from my own little faction,
And when I fell in with His Worship one day
In our talk the same topic came up by the way.
'If', said he, 'I found fault, pure good-will was the cause,
And my duty to point out religion's strict laws.'
—'Not at all', I responded, 'I make no complaint,
As a neighbour of mine you need feel no constraint;
In your presence I am, as my bent head declares,
Metamorphosed at once from gay youth to grey hairs,
And if my true nature eludes your analysis,
Your claim to omniscience need fear no paralysis;
For me also my nature remains still enravelled,
The sea of my thoughts is too deep and untravelled:
I too long to know the Iqbal of reality,
And often shed tears at this wall of duality.
To Iqbal of Iqbal little knowledge is given;
I say this not jesting—not jesting, by Heaven!'

مجموعۂ اضداد ہے، اقبالؔ نہیں ہے

دل دفترِ حکمت ہے، طبیعت خفقانی

رندی سے بھی آگاہ، شریعت سے بھی واقف

پوچھو جو تصوف کی، تو منصور کا ثانی

اس شخص کی ہم پر تو حقیقت نہیں کھلتی

ہوگا یہ کسی اور ہی اسلام کا بانی

القصہ بہت طول دیا وعظ کو اپنے

تا دیر رہی آپ کی یہ نغز بیانی

اس شہر میں جو بات ہو، اُڑ جاتی ہے سب میں

میں نے بھی سنی اپنے احبّا کی زبانی

اک دن جو سرِ راہ ملے حضرتِ زاہد

پھر چھڑ گئی باتوں میں وہی بات پُرانی

فرمایا، شکایت وہ محبت کے سبب تھی

تھا فرض مِرا راہ شریعت کی دِکھانی

میں نے یہ کہا کوئی گِلہ مجھ کو نہیں ہے

یہ آپ کا حق تھا زرہِ قُربِ مکانی

خم ہے سرِ تسلیم مِرا آپ کے آگے

پیری ہے تواضع کے سبب میری جوانی

گر آپ کو معلوم نہیں میری حقیقت

پیدا نہیں کچھ اس سے قصورِ ہمہ دانی

میں خود بھی نہیں اپنی حقیقت کا شناسا

گہرا ہے مِرے بحرِ خیالات کا پانی

مجھ کو بھی تمنا ہے کہ اقبالؔ کو دیکھوں

کی اس کی جدائی میں بہت اشک فشانی

اقبالؔ بھی 'اقبالؔ' سے آگاہ نہیں ہے

کچھ اس میں تمسخر نہیں، واللہ نہیں ہے

5. *The Moon*

My desert from your native land how many a league divides!
Yet by your power the waters of my heart feel these rough tides.
To what far gathering are you bound, from what far gathering
        come?
Your face is blanched, as if from journeyings long and
        wearisome.
You in this universe all light, and I all darkness, share
One destiny together in our valley of despair;
I burn in a flame of longing, ah ! burn for the gift of sight,
And you, all seared with fires of longing, beg the sun for light;
And if your footsteps cannot stray from one fixed circle's bound,
I too move in one circle as a compass-hand moves round.
You roam forlorn life's path to whose dull griefs I too am
        doomed,
You shining through creation's throng, I in my flame consumed;
A long road lies before me and a long road waits for you;
The silence of your thronging skies is here in my heart too.
My nature is like yours, you who were born to seek, to rove,
Though yours are silver rays—the light that guides my feet is
        love.
I too dwell among many : if you go companionless
Amid the company of heaven, I know your loneliness;
And when for you the blaze of dawn proclaims extinction, I
Drown with you in the crystal glory of eternity.
And yet, yet, radiant moon! we are not of one race ; it is
No heart like your heart that can feel and tell its miseries.
Though you are all of light, and I of darkness made, you are
Still far from thirst of consciousness, a thousand journeys far;
Before my soul the path lies clear in view that it must trace—
No gleam of knowledge such as mine will ever light your face.

چاند

میرے ویرانے سے کوسوں دور ہے تیرا وطن
قصد کس محفل کا ہے؟ آتا ہے کس محفل سے تو؟

آفرینش میں سراپا نور تو، ظلمت ہوں میں
آہ! میں جلتا ہوں سوزِ اشتیاقِ دید سے

ایک حلقے پر اگر قائم تری رفتار ہے
زندگی کی رہ میں سرگرداں ہے تو، حیراں ہوں میں

میں رہِ منزل میں ہوں، تو بھی رہِ منزل میں ہے
تُو طلب خو ہے، تو میرا بھی یہی دستور ہے

انجمن ہے ایک میری بھی جہاں رہتا ہوں میں
مہر کا پرتو ترے حق میں ہے پیغامِ اجل

پھر بھی اے ماہِ مبیں! میں اور ہوں تو اور ہے
گرچہ میں ظلمت سراپا ہوں، سراپا نور تو

جو مری ہستی کا مقصد ہے، مجھے معلوم ہے

ہے مگر دریائے دل تیری کشش سے موجزن
زرد رُو شاید ہوا رنجِ رہِ منزل سے تو؟

اس سیہ روزی پہ لیکن تیرا ہم قسمت ہوں میں
تو سراپا سوز داغِ منتِ خورشید سے

میری گردش بھی مثالِ گردشِ پرکار ہے
تو فروزاں محفلِ ہستی میں ہے، سوزاں ہوں میں

تیری محفل میں جو خاموشی ہے، میرے دل میں ہے
چاندنی ہے نور تیرا، عشق میرا نور ہے

بزم میں اپنی اگر یکتا ہے تُو، تنہا ہوں میں
محو کر دیتا ہے مجھ کو جلوۂ حسنِ ازل

درد جس پہلو سے اُٹھتا ہو، وہ پہلو اور ہے
سیکڑوں منزل ہے ذوقِ آگہی سے دور تو

یہ چمک وہ ہے، جبیں جس سے تری محروم ہے!

6. Morning Star

ENOUGH of this sun-and-moon-neighbouring glory—
Enough of this office of heralding dawn!
Worthless to me the abodes of the planets,
Lowly earth-dwelling is more than these heights
I inhabit, no heaven but a realm of extinction,
Dawn's skirt of the hundred-fold rent for my shroud:
To live, to die daily my fate, to be poured
The morning-draught first by the cupbearer Death.
Thankless this duty, this station, this dignity—
Better the dark than to shine for one hour!

No star would I be, if it lay in my will,
But a gleaming white pearl in the cavernous sea,
And then, if too fearful the strife of the waves,
Leave ocean, and hang in some necklace—what joy
It would be there to glitter as beauty's bright pendent,
A gem in the crown of an emperor's consort!
What fragment of stone, if its destiny smiled,
Might not flash in the ring on the finger of Solomon?
But glory of all such in this world must vanish,
The rich gem must vanish at last. That alone
Lives, that need have no acquaintance with death:
Can that be called life, that hears death's importunity?
If, making earth lovely, our end must be thus,
Let me rather be changed to a flower-falling dewdrop,

صبح کا ستارہ

لطفِ ہمسائیگی شمس و قمر کو چھوڑوں   اور اس خدمتِ پیغامِ سحر کو چھوڑوں

میرے حق میں تو نہیں تاروں کی بستی اچھی   اس بلندی سے زمیں والوں کی پستی اچھی

آساں کیا، عدم آباد وطن ہے میرا   صبح کا دامنِ صد چاک کفن ہے میرا

میری قسمت میں ہے ہر روز کا مرنا جینا   ساقیِ موت کے ہاتھوں سے صبُوحی پینا

نہ یہ خدمت، نہ یہ عزت، نہ یہ رفعت اچھی   اس گھڑی بھر کے چمکنے سے تو ظلمت اچھی

میری قدرت میں جو ہوتا، تو نہ اختر بنتا

قعرِ دریا میں چمکتا ہوا گوہر بنتا

واں بھی موجوں کی کشاکش سے جو دل گھبراتا   چھوڑ کر بحر، کہیں زیب گلو ہو جاتا

ہے چمکنے میں مزا حسن کا زیور بن کر   زینتِ تاجِ سرِ بانوئے قیصر بن کر

ایک پتھر کے جو ٹکڑے کا نصیبا جاگا   خاتمِ دستِ سلیماں کا نگیں بن کے رہا

ایسی چیزوں کا مگر دہر میں ہے کام شکست   ہے گہر ہائے گراں مایہ کا انجام شکست

زندگی وہ ہے کہ جو ہو نہ شناسائے اجل   کیا وہ جینا ہے کہ ہو جس میں تقاضائے اجل

ہے یہ انجام اگر زینتِ عالم ہو کر   کیوں نہ گر جاؤں کسی پھول پہ شبنم ہو کر؟

A speck in the gold-dust that paints a bride's forehead,
A spark in the sigh that a wounded heart breathes—
Or why not the glistening tear-drop that rolls
Down the long lashes fringing the eyes of a lady
Whose lord, in chain armour enmeshed, must set forth
To the battlefield, hurried by love of his country,
—A woman whose face like a picture shows hope
And despair side by side, and whose silence shames speech:
Her patient thoughts built on her husband's firm soul,
Her looks from their modesty borrowing eloquence,
That hour of farewell when the rosy cheek pales
And the sorrow of parting makes beauty more beautiful!
There, though she locked up her heart, I would gleam,
One waterdrop spilt from her eye's brimming cup,
To find in the dust an immortal new life,
And teach to the world the long passion of love.

کسی پیشانی کے افشاں کے ستاروں میں رہوں
اشک بن کر سرِ مژگاں سے اٹک جاؤں میں
جس کا شوہر ہو رواں، ہو کے زرہ میں مستور
یاس و اُمید کا نظارہ جو دکھلاتی ہو
جس کو شوہر کی رضا تابِ شکیبائی دے
زرد، رخصت کی گھڑی، عارضِ گلگوں ہوجائے
لاکھ وہ ضبط کرے پر میں ٹپک ہی جاؤں

کسی مظلوم کی آہوں کے شراروں میں رہوں
کیوں نہ اُس بیوی کی آنکھوں سے ٹپک جاؤں میں
سوئے میدانِ وغا، حُبِّ وطن سے مجبور
جس کی خاموشی سے تقریر بھی شرماتی ہو
اور نگاہوں کو حیا طاقتِ گویائی دے
کششِ حُسنِ غمِ ہجر سے افزوں ہوجائے
ساغرِ دیدۂ پُرنم سے چھلک ہی جاؤں

خاک میں مل کے حیاتِ ابدی پاجاؤں
عشق کا سوز زمانے کو دِکھاتا جاؤں

7. A New Altar

I'LL tell you truth, oh Brahmin, if I may make so bold!
These idols in your temples—these idols have grown old;
To hate your fellow-mortals is all they teach you, while
Our God too sets His preachers to scold and to revile;
Sickened, from both your temple and our shrine I have run,
Alike our preachers' sermons and your fond myths I shun.
—In every graven image you fancied God: I see
In each speck of my country's poor dust, divinity.

Come, let us life suspicion's thick curtains once again,
Unite once more the sundered, wipe clean division's stain.
Too long has lain deserted the heart's warm habitation—
Come, build here in our homeland an altar's new foundation,
And raise a spire more lofty than any of this globe,
With high pinnacles touching the hem of heaven's robe!
And there at every sunrise let our sweet chanting move
The hearts of all who worship, pouring them wine of love:
Firm strength, calm peace, shall blend in the hymns the votary
    sings—
For from love comes salvation to all earth's living things.

نیا شوالا

سچ کہہ دوں اے برہمن! گر تُو بُرا نہ مانے تیرے صنم کدوں کے بُت ہوگئے پرانے

اپنوں سے بَیر رکھنا تو نے بُتوں سے سیکھا جنگ و جدل سکھایا واعظ کو بھی خدا نے

تنگ آکے میں نے آخر دَیر و حرم کو چھوڑا واعظ کا وعظ چھوڑا، چھوڑے ترے فسانے

پتھر کی مورتوں میں سمجھا ہے تُو خدا ہے

خاکِ وطن کا مجھ کو ہر ذرّہ دیوتا ہے

آ، غیریت کے پردے اک بار پھر اُٹھادیں بچھڑوں کو پھر ملادیں، نقشِ دوئی مٹادیں

سُونی پڑی ہوئی ہے مدت سے دل کی بستی آ، اک نیا شوالا اس دیس میں بنادیں

دنیا کے تیرتھوں سے اونچا ہو اپنا تیرتھ دامانِ آسماں سے اس کا کلس ملادیں

ہر صبح اُٹھ کے گائیں منتر وہ میٹھے میٹھے سارے پجاریوں کو مے پِیت کی پلادیں

شکتی بھی، شانتی بھی، بھگتوں کے گیت میں ہے

دھرتی کے باسیوں کی مُکتی پریت میں ہے

8. *On the Bank of the Ravi*

RAPT in its music, in evening's hush, the Ravi;
But how it is with this heart, do not ask—
Hearing in these soft cadences a prayer-call,
Seeing all earth God's precinct, here beside
The margin of the onward-flowing waters
Standing I scarcely know where I am standing.

With palsied hand the taverner of heaven
Has brought the cup: red wine stains evening's skirt;
Day's headlong caravan has made haste towards
Extinction: twilight smoulders like hot ash
Of the sun's funeral pyre. In solitude
Far off, magnificent, those towers stand, where
The flower of Moghul chivalry lies asleep;
A legend of Time's tyranny is that palace;
A book, the register of days gone by;
No mansion, but a melody of silence—
No trees, but an unspeaking parliament.
Swiftly across the river's bosom glides
A boat, the oarsman wrestling with the waves,
A skiff light-motioned as a darting glance,
Soon far beyond the eye's curved boundary.
So glides the bark of mortal life, in the ocean
Of eternity so born, so vanishing,
Yet never knowing what is death; for it
May disappear from sight, but cannot perish.

کنارِ راوی

سکوتِ شام میں محوِ سرود ہے راوی
نہ پوچھ مجھ سے جو ہے کیفیت مرے دل کی

پیامِ سجدے کا یہ زیرو بم ہُوا مجھ کو
جہاں تمام سوادِ حرم ہُوا مجھ کو

سرِ کنارۂ آبِ رواں کھڑا ہوں میں
خبر نہیں مجھے کہاں کھڑا ہوں میں

شرابِ سُرخ سے رنگیں ہُوا ہے دامنِ شام
لیے ہے پیرِ فلک دستِ رعشہ دار میں جام

عدم کو قافلۂ روز تیز گام چلا
شفق نہیں ہے، یہ سورج کے پھول ہیں گویا

کھڑے ہیں دُور وہ عظمت فزائے تنہائی
منارِ خواب گہہ شہسوارِ چغتائی

فسانۂ ستمِ انقلاب ہے یہ محل
کوئی زمانِ سلف کی کتاب ہے یہ محل

مقام کیا ہے، سرودِخموش ہے گویا
شجر، یہ انجمنِ بے خروش ہے گویا

رواں ہے سینۂ دریا پہ اک سفینۂ تیز
ہُوا ہے موج سے ملاح جس کا گرمِ ستیز

سبک روی میں ہے مثلِ نگاہ یہ کشتی
نکل کے حلقۂ حدِّ نظر سے دُور گئی

جہازِ زندگیٔ آدمی ہے یُونہی رواں
ابد کے بحر میں پیدا یُونہی، نہاں ہے یُونہیں

شکست سے یہ کبھی آشنا نہیں ہوتا
نظر سے چھپتا ہے، لیکن فنا نہیں ہوتا

9. *Beauty's Essence.*

BEAUTY asked God one day
This question: 'Why
Didst Thou not make me, in Thy world, undying?'
And God replying—
'A picture-show is this world: all this world
A tale out of the long night of not-being;
And in it, seeing
Its nature works through mutability,
That only is lovely whose essence knows decay.'

The moon stood near and heard this colloquy,
The words took wing about the sky
And reached the morning-star;
Dawn learned them from its star, and told the dew—
It told the heavens' whisper to
Earth's poor familiar;
And at the dew's report the flower's eye filled,
With pain the new bud's tiny heartbeat thrilled;
Springtime fled from the garden, weeping;
Youth, that had come to wander there, went creeping
Sadly away.

حقیقتِ حُسن

جہاں میں کیوں نہ مجھے تُو نے لازوال کیا	خدا سے حُسن نے اک روز یہ سوال کیا
شبِ درازِ عدم کا فسانہ ہے دنیا	ملا جواب کہ تصویر خانہ ہے دنیا
وہی حسیں ہے حقیقت زوال ہے جس کی	ہوئی ہے رنگِ تغیّر سے جب نمود اس کی
فلک پہ عام ہوئی، اخترِ سحر نے سُنی	کہیں قریب تھا، یہ گفتگو قمر نے سُنی
فلک کی بات بتادی زمیں کے محرم کو	سحر نے تارے سے سُن کر سُنائی شبنم کو
کلی کا نتھّا سا دل خون ہوگیا غم سے	بھر آئے پُھول کے آنسو پیامِ شبنم سے
شباب سیر کو آیا تھا، سوگوار گیا!	چمن سے روتا ہوا موسمِ بہار گیا

10. Moon and Stars

TREMBLING at the chill breath of dawn
The fearful stars said to the moon:
'About us lies heaven's changeless scene
Where wearied we must shine, still shine,
Tasked to move on, on, morn and eve—
To move, to move, for ever move!
No creature of this world knows rest,
Nowhere can fabled peace exist,
All things condemned by tyrant laws
To wander, stars, men, rocks, and trees—
But shall this journeying ever end,
Ever a destination find?'

'Oh my companions,' said the moon,
'You who night's harvest-acres glean,
On motion all this world's life hangs:
Such is the ancient doom of things.
Swift runs the shadowy steed of time
Lashed by desire's whip into foam,
And there's no loitering on that path,
For hidden in repose lurks death:
They that press on win clear—the late,
The laggard, trampled underfoot.
And what the goal of all this haste?—
Its cradle love, beauty its quest.'

چاند اور تارے

تارے کہنے لگے قمر سے
ہم تھک بھی گئے چمک چمک کر
چلنا، چلنا، مدام چلنا
کہتے ہیں جسے سکوں، نہیں ہے
تارے، انساں، شجر، حجر سب

ڈرتے ڈرتے دمِ سحر سے
نظارے رہے وہی فلک پر
کام اپنا ہے صبح و شام چلنا
بے تاب ہے اس جہاں کی ہر شے
رہتے ہیں ستم کش سفر سب
ہوگا کبھی ختم یہ سفر کیا؟
منزل کبھی آئے گی نظر کیا؟

اے مزرعِ شب کے خوشہ چینو!
یہ رسم قدیم ہے یہاں کی
کھا کھا کے طلب کا تازیانہ
پوشیدہ قرار میں اجل ہے
جو ٹھہرے ذرا، کچل گئے ہیں
آغاز ہے عشق، انتہا حُسن

کہنے لگا چاند، ہم نشینو!
جنبش سے ہے زندگی جہاں کی
ہے دوڑتا اشہبِ زمانہ
اس رہ میں مقام بے محل ہے
چلنے والے نکل گئے ہیں
انجام ہے اس خرام کا حُسن

11. One Evening

(By the Neckar at Heidelberg)

SILENT is the moonlight pale,
The boughs of all the trees are still,
The music-maker of the vale
Hushed, and the green robes of the hill;
Fallen into a swoon creation
Sleeps in the bosom of the night,
And from this hush such magic grows,
No more now Neckar's current flows;
Silent the starry caravan moves
Onward, no bell tinkling its flight,
Silent the hills and streams and groves,
All Nature lost in contemplation.
Oh heart, you to be silent: keep
      Your grief hugged close, and sleep.

ایک شام

(دریائے نیکر، ہائیڈل برگ، کے کنارے پر)

شاخیں ہیں خموش ہر شجر کی	خاموش ہے چاندنی قمر کی
کہسار کے سبز پوش خاموش	وادی کے نوا فروش خاموش
آغوش میں شب کے سوگئی ہے	فطرت بے ہوش ہوگئی ہے
نیکر کا خرام بھی سکوں سے	کچھ ایسا سکوت کا فسوں ہے
یہ قافلہ بے درار رواں ہے	تاروں کا خموش کارواں ہے
قدرت ہے مراقبے میں گویا	خاموش ہیں کوہ و دشت و دریا

اے دل! تو بھی خموش ہوجا

آغوش میں غم کو لے کے سوجا

12. Solitude

SOLITUDE, night—what pang is here?
Are not the stars your comrades? Clear
Majesty of those silent skies,
Drowsed earth, deep silence of the world,
That moon, that wilderness and hill—
White rose-beds all creation fill.
Sweet are the teardrops that have pearled
Like gleaming gems, like stars, your eyes;
But what thing do you crave? All Nature,
Oh my heart, is your fellow-creature.

تنہائی

انجم نہیں تیرے ہم نشیں کیا؟	تنہائی شب میں ہے حزیں کیا؟
خوابیدہ زمیں، جہانِ خاموش	یہ رفعتِ آسمانِ خاموش
فطرت ہے تمام نسترن زار	یہ چاند، یہ دشت و در، یہ کہسار
یعنی، ترے آنسوؤں کے تارے	موتی خوش رنگ، پیارے پیارے

کس شے کی تجھے ہوں ہے اے دل!

قدرت تری ہم نفس ہے اے دل!

13. Sicily

Now weep blood, oh eyes, for the tomb of the arts of Arabia
      stands there in sight
Where the men of the desert whose ships made a playground of
      ocean once rushed to the fight—
They who brought into emperors' thronerooms the earthquake,
      and swords in which lightnings had nested:
Their advent proclaimed a new world—till the old was devoured
      their keen blades never rested;
At their thundered *Arise!* a dead earth sprang to life, and man
      burst from the chains of unreason:
From that tumult our ears are still tingling with joy—shall their
      hymn never know a new season?

Oh Sicily, crown of the sea, like a guide in the waters' wide
      wilderness set,
On ocean's cheek rest like a dimple, rejoice with your lamps the
      wave-wanderer yet!
May your balm to the traveller's eye, the foam-dance on your
      rocks, be for ever the same—
You who cradled the arts of that nation whose earth-melting
      lustre once shone like a flame!

As the nightingale-voice of Shiraz for Baghdad, and for Delhi
      Dagh shed bitter tears,
As Ibn Badrun's soul lamented when heaven ended Granada's
      opulent years,

صِقلیہ
(جزیرۂ سِسلی)

رولے اب دل کھول کر اے دیدۂ خونناب بار!
تھا یہاں ہنگامہ ان صحرا نشینوں کا کبھی
زلزلے جن سے شہنشاہوں کے درباروں میں تھے
اک جہانِ تازہ کا پیغام تھا جن کا ظہور
مردہ عالَم زندہ جن کی شورشِ قُم سے ہوا
غلغلوں سے جس کے لذّت گیراب تک گوش ہے
آہ! اے سِسلی! سمندر کی ہے تجھ سے آبرو
زیب تیرے خال سے رُخسار دریا کو رہے
ہو سبک چشم مسافر پر ترا منظر مدام
تو کبھی اُس قوم کی تہذیب کا گہوارہ تھا
نالہ کش شیراز کا بلبل ہوا بغداد پر
آسماں نے دولتِ غرناطہ جب برباد کی

وہ نظر آتا ہے تہذیبِ حجازی کا مزار!
بحر بازی گاہ تھا جن کے سفینوں کا کبھی
بجلیوں کے آشیانے جن کی تلواروں میں تھے
کھا گئی عصرِ کہن کو جن کی تیغِ ناصبور
آدمی آزاد زنجیر توہّم سے ہوا
کیا وہ تکبیر اب ہمیشہ کے لیے خاموش ہے؟
رہنما کی طرح اس پانی کے صحرا میں ہے تو
تیری شمعوں سے تسلّی بحر پیما کو رہے
موج رقصاں تیرے ساحل کی چٹانوں پر مدام
حسنِ عالم سوز جس کا آتشِ نظّارہ تھا
داغِ رویا خون کے آنسو جہان آباد پر
ابنِ بدروں کے دلِ ناشاد نے فریاد کی

So to sorrow with you fate has chosen Iqbal, oh this heart that
    knows your heart so well!
Whose annals lie lost in your ruins?—those shores and their
    echoless music might tell.
Tell your grief then to me, who am grief, who am dust of that
    caravan whose magnet you were:
Stir my veins—let the picture glow bright with fresh colour,
    the ancient days' record declare!
I go with your gift to the Indies, and I who weep here will make
    others weep there.

غم نصیب اقبالؔ کو بخشا گیا ماتم ترا

چن لیا تقدیر نے وہ دل کہ تھا محرم ترا

ہے ترے آثار میں پوشیدہ کس کی داستاں؟

تیرے ساحل کی خموشی میں ہے اندازِ بیاں

درد اپنا مجھ سے کہہ، میں بھی سراپا درد ہوں

جس کی تو منزل تھا، میں اُس کارواں کی گرد ہوں

رنگ تصویرِ کہن میں بھر کے دکھلا دے مجھے

قصہ ایامِ سلف کا کہہ کے تڑپا دے مجھے

میں ترا تحفہ سوئے ہندوستاں لے جاؤں گا

خود یہاں روتا ہوں، اوروں کو وہاں رُلواؤں گا

14. Two Planets

Two planets meeting face to face,
One to the other cried 'How sweet
If endlessly we might embrace,
And here for ever stay! how sweet
If Heaven a little might relent,
And leave our light in one light blent!'

But through that longing to dissolve
In one, the parting summons sounded.
Immutably the stars revolve,
By changeless orbits each is bounded;
Eternal union is a dream,
And severance the world's law supreme.

دوستارے

آئے جو قِراں میں دو ستارے   کہنے لگا ایک، دوسرے سے

یہ وصل مدام ہو تو کیا خوب   انجامِ خرام ہو تو کیا خوب

تھوڑا سا جو مہرباں فلک ہو

ہم دونوں کی ایک ہی چمک ہو

لیکن یہ وصال کی تمنّا   پیغامِ فراق تھی سراپا

گردشِ تاروں کا ہے مقدّر   ہر ایک کی راہ ہے مقرّر

ہے خواب ثباتِ آشنائی

آئینِ جہاں کا ہے جدائی

15. On a Flower-offering

WHEN she walks drunk with pride
About the garden path,
Flowerets on every side
Lift up one suppliant voice—
May she, ah God, make me
Of all the rest her choice,
Raise me from low degree
To wake the sunflower's wrath!
—Divine fortune, that she
Should pluck *you* from the stem!
Your rivals toss their petals;
The shock of severance past,
New bliss of union settles
Upon your life, whose gem
Shines perfectly at last.

My heart, though it found love
In feeling hearts its vassal—
This heart of mine, pride of
The garden of my youth,
Could never flower-like nestle
In the desired one's breast,
Nor ever feel the smooth
Touch of the shimmering vest.
No springtime shall come freighting
Its leaves with April's luck,
It withers in this waiting
For her who comes to pluck.

پھُول کا تحفہ عطا ہونے پر

وہ مستِ ناز جو گلشن میں جانکلتی ہے   کلی کلی کی زباں سے دُعا نکلتی ہے

"الٰہی! پھولوں میں وہ انتخاب مجھ کو کرے

کلی سے رشکِ گُلِ آفتاب مجھ کو کرے"

تجھے وہ شاخ سے توڑیں! از ہے نصیب ترے   تڑپتے رہ گئے گلزار میں رقیب ترے

اُٹھا کے صدمۂ فرقت وصال تک پہنچا   تری حیات کا جوہر کمال تک پہنچا

مرا کنول کہ تصدّق ہیں جس پہ اہلِ نظر   مرے شباب کے گلشن کو ناز ہے جس پر

کبھی یہ پھول ہم آغوشِ مدّعا نہ ہوا   کسی کے دامنِ رنگیں سے آشنا نہ ہوا

شگفتہ کر نہ سکے گی کبھی بہار اسے

فسردہ رکھتا ہے گلچیں کا انتظار اسے

16. *Before the Prophet's Throne*

S<small>ICK</small> of this world and all this world's tumult
I who had lived fettered to dawn and sunset,
Yet never fathomed the planet's hoary laws,
Taking provision for my way set out
From earth, and angels led me where the Prophet
Holds audience, and before the mercy-seat.
  'Nightingale of the gardens of Hejaz! each bud
  Is melting', said those Lips, 'in your song's passion-flood;
  Your heart forever steeped in the wine of ecstasy,
  Your reeling feet nobler than any suppliant knee.
  But since, taught by these Seraphim to mount so high,
  You have soared up from nether realms towards the sky
  And like a scent come here from the orchards of the earth—
  What do you bring for us, what is your offering worth?'

'Master! there is no quiet in that land of time and space,
Where the existence that we crave hides and still hides its face;
Though all creation's flowerbeds teem with tulip and red rose,
The flower whose perfume is true love—that flower no garden
  knows.
But I have brought this chalice here to make my sacrifice;
The thing it holds you will not find in all your Paradise.
See here, oh Lord, the honour of your people brimming up!
The martyred blood of Tripoli, oh Lord, is in this cup.'

حضورِ رسالت مآبﷺ میں

گراں جو مجھ پہ یہ ہنگامۂ زمانہ ہوا 　　　 جہاں سے باندھ کے رختِ سفر روانہ ہوا

قیودِ شام و سحر میں بسر تو کی، لیکن 　　　 نظام کہنۂ عالم سے آشنا نہ ہوا

فرشتے بزمِ رسالتؐ میں لے گئے مجھ کو

حضور آیۂ رحمتؐ میں لے گئے مجھ کو

کہا حضورؐ نے، اے عندلیبِ باغِ حجاز! 　　　 کلی کلی ہے تری گرمیٔ نوا سے گداز

ہمیشہ سرخوشِ جامِ ولا ہے دل تیرا 　　　 فتادگی ہے تری غیرتِ سجودِ نیاز

اُڑا جو پستیٔ دنیا سے تو سوئے گردوں 　　　 سکھائی تجھ کو ملائک نے رفعتِ پرواز

نکل کے باغِ جہاں سے برنگِ بو آیا

ہمارے واسطے کیا تحفہ لے کے تُو آیا؟

''حضورؐ! دہر میں آسودگی نہیں ملتی 　　　 تلاش جس کی ہے وہ زندگی نہیں ملتی

ہزاروں لالہ و گل ہیں ریاضِ ہستی میں 　　　 وفا کی جس میں ہو بو، وہ کلی نہیں ملتی

مگر میں نذر کو اک آبگینہ لایا ہوں 　　　 جو چیز اس میں ہے، جنت میں بھی نہیں ملتی

جھلکتی ہے تری اُمت کی آبرو اس میں

طرابلس کے شہیدوں کا ہے لہو اس میں''

17. I and You

In me no mind of Moses, in you no virtue
Of Abraham: idolatrous foes like theirs,
New Samris, Azars, have with eldritch arts
Destroyed us; I am a song burned out in the throat,
And you a shrivelled colour, a frightened scent;
I, memory of the pain of longing—you,
Echo of a lament for love. My joys
Are gall, my honey venom, my soul twin-brother
To blank oblivion: your heart's temple pawned
To Persia's strange gods, your religion bartered

To infidels. Life's every breath is numbered—
To count them, terror: to wail at life's brief span,
Poison; do not bewail that terror, do not
Swallow the poison of that wailing; take
The road by which the saints came to their crown,
And have no thought, if one spark burns in your dust,
Of wealth or penury; for here on earth
Black peasant bread breeds Haidar's strength. Oh lamp
Of the shrine! teach me, your circling moth, a way
Of worship to renew in me that nature
Which like the salamander feeds on flame.
Against the guardians of the shrine, the shrine
Brings accusation of such villainy
Decked out as loyal zeal, that let me once
Proclaim it in the very idol-house,
The senseless monsters would cry out 'Oh Vishnu,
Vishnu!' Not new to-day the world's arena,
Not new the antagonists, face to face, hands clenched;
Unchanged of purpose stands the Lion of God,
Unchanged the opposing champions. Aid us, Prophet,
Lord of Arabia and the alien lands!
Awaiting here thy bounty are those beggars
Whom thou has given the pride of Alexander.

میں اور تُو

نہ سلیقہ مجھ میں کلیم کا، نہ قرینہ تجھ میں خلیل کا
میں ہلاکِ جادوئے سامری، تو قتیلِ شیوہ ٔ آزری

میں نوائے سوختہ درگلو، تو پریدہ رنگ، رمیدہ بو
میں حکایتِ غم آرزو، تو حدیثِ ماتم دلبری

مرا عیش غم، مرا شہد سم، مری بو دہم نفسِ عدم
ترا دل حرم، گردِ عجم، ترا دیں خریدہ ٔ کافری!

دمِ زندگی رمِ زندگی، غمِ زندگی سمِ زندگی
غم رم نہ کر، سم غم نہ کھا کہ یہی ہے شانِ قلندری!

تری خاک میں ہے اگر شررتو خیالِ فقر و غنا نہ کر
کہ جہاں میں نانِ شعیر پر ہے مدارِ قوتِ حیدری!

کوئی ایسی طرزِ طواف تو مجھے اے چراغِ حرم بتا!
کہ ترے پتنگ کو پھر عطا ہو وہی سرشتِ سمندری!

گلہ ٔ جفائے وفا نما کہ حرم کو اہلِ حرم سے ہے
کسی بتکدے میں بیاں کروں تو کہے صنم بھی تہری ہری

نہ ستیزہ گاہ جہاں نئی، نہ حریفِ پنجہ فگن نئے
وہی فطرتِ اسد اللّٰہی، وہی مرتبیٰ، وہی عنتری

کرم اے شہِ عرب و عجم کہ کھڑے ہیں منتظرِ کرم
وہ گدا کہ تو نے عطا کیا ہے جنھیں دماغِ سکندری

18. Khizar, the Guide

(1) THE POET

By the river's brink I stood one evening, lost in the scene,
Yet hiding a world of fretting thoughts in my heart's cell.
Night deepened silence: calm the air, languid the current,
River or painted water the eye could scarcely tell.
As the sucking infant laid in the cradle falls asleep
The restless wave lay slumberously in its deep well,
The birds held captive by night's gramarye in their nests,
And the faint-bleaming stars fast bound by the bright moon's
      spell.
There that world-measuring courier I had sight of—Khizar,
That ancient in whom youth's colours fresh as the daybreak
      dwell.
'Seeker', said he, 'of eternal secrets! when the heart
Sees with clear vision, the fates that rule earth wear no veil.'
At these words in my soul doomed to long search awoke
A tumult as of Judgment Day; and thus I spoke.

'To your world-ranging eye is visible the storm
Whose fury yet lies in tranquil sleep under the sea:
That innocent life,—that poor man's boat,—that wall of the
      orphan,
Taught Moses' wisdom to stand before yours wonderingly!

خضرِ راہ
شاعر

ساحلِ دریا پہ میں اک رات تھا محوِ نظر

گوشئہ دل میں چھپائے اک جہانِ اضطراب

شب سکوت افزا، ہوا آسودہ، دریا نرم سیر

تھی نظر حیراں کہ یہ دریا ہے یا تصویرِ آب!

جیسے گہوارے میں سوجاتا ہے طفلِ شیرخوار

موج مضطر تھی کہیں گہرائیوں میں مستِ خواب!

رات کے افسوں سے طائرِ آشیانوں میں اسیر

انجم کم ضو گرفتارِ طلسمِ ماہتاب!

دیکھتا کیا ہوں کہ وہ پیکِ جہاں پیما خضر

جس کی پیری میں ہے ماندِ سحر رنگِ شباب

کہہ رہا ہے مجھ سے، اے جویائے اسرارِ ازل!

چشمِ دل وا ہو تو ہے تقدیرِ عالم بے حجاب!

دل میں یہ سن کر بپا ہنگامئہ محشر ہوا

میں شہیدِ جستجو تھا، یوں سخن گستر ہوا

اے تری چشمِ جہاں بیں پر وہ طوفاں آشکار

جن کے ہنگامے ابھی دریا میں سوتے ہیں خموش

'کشتئ مسکیں' و 'جانِ پاک' و 'دیوارِ یتیم'

علمِ موسیٰ بھی ہے تیرے سامنے حیرت فروش

You shun abodes, for desert-roaming, for ways that know
No day or night, from yesterdays and to-morrows free.
—What is the riddle of life? What thing is the State? or why
Must labour and capital so bloodily disagree?
Asia's time-honoured cloak grows ragged and wears out,
From upstart lands her young men borrow their finery;
Though Alexander could never find the elixir of life,
His robber spirit still revels here in drunken glee;
The lord of Mecca barters the honour of Mecca's faith
That the stubborn Turk, late convert, guards through war's
        agony.
Tyrants and flames once more on Abraham's race have glared:
For whom this new ordeal, or by whose hand prepared?'

چھوڑ کر آبادیاں رہتا ہے تو صحرانورد
زندگی تیری ہے بے روز و شب و فردا و دوش

زندگی کا راز کیا ہے؟ سلطنت کیا چیز ہے؟
اور یہ سرمایہ و محنت میں ہے کیسا خروش؟

ہو رہا ہے ایشیا کا خرقۂ دیرینہ چاک
نوجواں اقوامِ نَو دولت کے ہیں پیرایہ پوش!

گرچہ اسکندر رہا محرومِ آبِ زندگی
فطرتِ اسکندری اب تک ہے گرم ناؤ نوش!

بیٹھتا ہے ہاشمی، ناموسِ دینِ مصطفیٰؐ
خاک و خوں میں مل رہا ہے ترکمانِ سخت کوش!

آگ ہے، اولادِ ابراہیمؑ ہے، نمرود ہے!
کیا کسی کو پھر کسی کا امتحاں مقصود ہے؟

Khizar's Reply

(2) DESERT-ROAMING

WHAT is it to make you wonder, if I roam the desert
    waste?
Witness of enduring life is this unending toil and haste!
You, shut in by walls, have never known that moment when
    the shrill
Bugle-call that sounds the march goes echoing over wood and
    hill,
Never known the wild deer's careless walk across its sandy
    plain,
Never halt unroofed, uncumbered, on the trail no milestones
    chain,
Never fleeting vision of that star that crowns the daybreak hour,
Never Gabriel's radiant brow effulgent from heaven's topmost
    tower,
Nor the going-down of suns in stillnesses of desert ways,
Twilight splendour such as brightened Abraham's world-
    beholding gaze,
Nor those springs of running water where the caravans take
    rest
As in heaven bright spirits cluster round the Fountain of the
    Blest!
Wildernesses ever new love's fever seeks and thirsts to roam—
You the furrowed field and palm-grove fetter tight to one poor
    home;
Mellow grows the wine of life when hand to hand the cup goes
    round
Foolish one! in this alone is life's eternal secret found.

جوابِ خضر

صحرانوردی

کیوں تعجب ہے مری صحرانوردی پر تجھے؟

یہ تگاپوئے دمادم زندگی کی ہے دلیل

اے رہینِ خانہ تو نے وہ سماں دیکھا نہیں

گونجتی ہے جب فضائے دشت میں بانگِ رحیل!

ریت کے ٹیلے پہ وہ آہو کا بے پروا خرام

وہ حضر بے برگ و ساماں، وہ سفر بے سنگ و میل!

وہ نمودِ اخترِ سیماب پا ہنگامِ صبح

یا نمایاں بامِ گردوں سے جبینِ جبریلؑ!

وہ سکوتِ شامِ صحرا میں غروبِ آفتاب

جس سے روشن تر ہوئی چشمِ جہاں بینِ خلیلؑ!

اور وہ پانی کے چشمے پر مقامِ کارواں

اہلِ ایماں جس طرح جنت میں گردِ سلسبیل!

تازہ ویرانے کی سودائے محبت کو تلاش

اور آبادی میں تو زنجیرئ کشت و نخیل!

پختہ تر ہے گردشِ پیہم سے جامِ زندگی

ہے یہی اے بے خبر رازِ دوامِ زندگی!

(3) THE STATE

WHAT Scripture sets forth riddlingly
    Of Kings, let me impart:
In towering empires sovereignty
    Is all a conjuror's art—

If ever subjects from their sleep
    Half rouse themselves, the sure
Enchantments of their rulers steep
    Their wits in dreams once more;

When Mahmud's blandishments begin
    Ayaz' slave-eyes dote,
And find a fine love-token in
    The halter round his throat.

But now the blood of Israel
    Boils up in rage at last,
And some new Moses breaks the spell
    That wizard Samri cast!

None with dominion's orb invest
    But the Most High alone:
He is the sovereign, all the rest
    Are idols carved from stone;

Stain with no slavery your free-souled
    Estate,—worse pagan than
The Brahmin, if your chisel mould
    A king out of a man.

سلطنت

آ بتاؤں تجھ کو رمزِ آیئہ اِنَّ الْمُلُوْک
سلطنت اقوامِ غالب کی ہے اک جادوگری

خواب سے بیدار ہوتا ہے ذرا محکوم اگر
پھر سلا دیتی ہے اُس کو حکمراں کی ساحری

جادوئے محمود کی تاثیر سے چشمِ ایاز
دیکھتی ہے حلقۂ گردن میں سازِ دلبری

خونِ اسرائیل آجاتا ہے آخر جوش میں
توڑ دیتا ہے کوئی موسیٰ طلسمِ سامری

سروری زیبا فقط اُس ذاتِ بے ہمتا کو ہے
حکمراں ہے اک وہی، باقی بتانِ آزری

از غلامی فطرتِ آزاد را رسوا مکن
تا تراشی خواجہ از برہمن کافر تری

In the West the people rule, they say:
        And what is this new reign?
The same harp still, the same strings play
        The despots' old refrain;

In Demos-dress let tyranny's
        Old demon-dance be seen,
Your fancy calls up Liberty's
        Blue-mantled fairy queen!

Those Parliaments and their reforms,
        Charters and Bills of Rights—
The Western pharmacopoeia swarms
        With opiate delights;

That rhetoric of the Senator,
        Flowing in fiery stream—
God save the mark! the brokers' war
        Of gold is its true theme.

This paint and perfume, this mirage,
        A garden's blooming face
You thought, simpleton, and your cage
        A downy nesting-place.

ہے وہی سازِ کہن مغرب کا جمہوری نظام

جس کے پردوں میں نہیں غیر از نوائے قیصری

دیوِ استبداد جمہوری قبا میں پائے کوب

تو سمجھتا ہے یہ آزادی کی ہے نیلم پری

مجلسِ آئین و اصلاح و رعایات و حقوق

طب مغرب میں مزے میٹھے، اثر خواب آوری!

گرمیٔ گفتارِ اعضائے مجالس الاماں!

یہ بھی اک سرمایہ داروں کی ہے جنگِ زرگری!

اس سرابِ رنگ و بو کو گلستاں سمجھا ہے تو

آہ! اے ناداں قفس کو آشیاں سمجھا ہے تو

(4) CAPITAL AND LABOUR

To the workman go, the toiler, and to him this message tell:
Words not mine alone, a message that the world's four corners
　　swell—
Oh, the crafty man of capital has devoured you flesh and fell:
On the wild deer's horns for ages your reward has run astray!
In the hand that forges all wealth he has dropped a grudging pay,
As the poor receive in charity what their betters throw away.
Like an Old Man of the Mountain he has fed you with hashish,
And poor innocent! you took it for the sweetest-flavoured
　　dish;
For the bourgeoisie is cunning, and from country and from
　　creed,
Colour, culture, caste and kingship, has brewed drugs to serve
　　its need;
For these false gods, witless victim, you have rushed upon your
　　doom
And been robbed of life's bright treasure for the taste of its mad
　　fume.
Your sharp paymasters have swept the board, they cheat and
　　know no shame:
You, forever unsuspecting, have forever lost the game.
But now come! for ways are changing in the assembly of the
　　earth,
And in Orient and in Occident your own age comes to birth!

For the lofty soul all ocean is too mean a gift: will you,
Like the careless bud, much longer be content with drops of dew?

سرمایہ و محنت

بندۂ مزدور کو جاکر مرا پیغام دے
خضر کا پیغام کیا، ہے یہ پیامِ کائنات
اے کہ تجھ کو کھا گیا سرمایہ دارِ حیلہ گر
شاخِ آہو پر رہی صدیوں تلک تیرے برات!
دستِ دولت آفریں کو مُزدیوں ملتی رہی
اہلِ ثروت جیسے دیتے ہیں غریبوں کو زکات
ساحرِ اَلمُوط نے تجھ کو دیا برگِ حشیش
اور تو اے بے خبر سمجھا اسے شاخِ نبات!
نسل، قومیت، کلیسا، سلطنت، تہذیب، رنگ
'خواجگی' نے خوب چن چن کے بنائے مُسکرات
کٹ مرا ناداں خیالی دیوتاؤں کے لیے
سُکر کی لذت میں تو لٹوا گیا نقدِ حیات
مکر کی چالوں سے بازی لے گیا سرمایہ دار
انتہائے سادگی سے کھا گیا مزدور مات
اُٹھ کہ اب بزمِ جہاں کا اور ہی انداز ہے
مشرق و مغرب میں تیرے دور کا آغاز ہے
ہمتِ عالی تو دریا بھی نہیں کرتی قبول
غنچہ ساں غافل ترے دامن میں شبنم کب تلک!

To those drowsy tales of Jamshed or Sikander for how long
Will you listen, now men's joy is in democracy's new song?
From the womb of this old universe a new red sun is born—
For extinguished stars, oh heaven, how much longer will you
     mourn?
Now the human mind has made of all its chains a broken heap,
For his banishment from Eden how much longer must Man
     weep?
How much longer, of the garden's old attendant asks the Spring,
For the red wounds of the rose your idle ointments will you
     bring?
Silly firefly, so long fluttering round the candle, now be free!
Where the lamp of your own spirit shines, there let your dwelling
     be.

نغمۂ بیداریٔ جمہور ہے سامانِ عیش

قصۂ خوابِ آورِ اسکندر و جم کب تلک

آفتابِ تازہ پیدا بطنِ گیتی سے ہوا

آسماں! ڈوبے ہوئے تاروں کا ماتم کب تلک!

توڑ ڈالیں فطرتِ انساں نے زنجیریں تمام

دوریٔ جنت سے روتی چشمِ آدم کب تلک

باغبانِ چارہ فرما سے یہ کہتی ہے بہار

زخمِ گل کے واسطے تدبیرِ مرہم کب تلک!

کرمکِ ناداں! طوافِ شمع سے آزاد ہو

اپنی فطرت کے تجلّی زار میں آباد ہو!

PART II

BAL-I-JIBRIL

GABRIEL'S WING

19. Ghazal No. 1

IF the stars wander from their path—is heaven mine, or Yours?
Should I care how the world goes? is the world then mine, or
    Yours?
If all eternity be void of passion's storms, whose fault,
God! that eternity should be so barren—mine, or Yours?
How could an Angel dare, in time's first dawning, to rebel?
Should I know that? whose confidant was Satan—mine, or
    Yours?
Gabriel is Yours, Muhammad Yours, Yours the Quran; yet in
Their gracious words, whose inmost soul is written—mine, or
    Yours?
And Man, that thing of dust, that star whose shining lights
    Your world—
To whose loss will it be if his race sicken: mine, or Yours?

غزل نمبر ۱

اگر کج رو ہیں انجم، آسماں تیرا ہے یا میرا؟   مجھے فکرِ جہاں کیوں ہو، جہاں تیرا ہے یا میرا؟

اگر ہنگامہ ہائے شوق سے ہے لامکاں خالی   خطا کس کی ہے یارب! لامکاں تیرا ہے یا میرا؟

اُسے صبحِ ازل انکار کی جرأت ہوئی کیوں کر؟   مجھے معلوم کیا! وہ رازداں تیرا ہے یا میرا؟

محمدؐ بھی ترا، جبریل بھی تیرا، قرآن بھی تیرا   مگر یہ حرفِ شیریں ترجماں تیرا ہے یا میرا؟

اسی کوکب کی تابانی سے ہے تیرا جہاں روشن

زوالِ آدمِ خاکی زیاں تیرا ہے یا میرا؟

20. Ghazal No. 2

HEAR my complaint and feel, or do not feel, with me:
He does not come to beg redress, whose soul walks free!
—Vast skies, and frozen winds, and man's one pinch of dust;
What urged You to create—kindness, or cruelty?
The garden breeze has shattered the rose's petalled tent:
Is this Your bounteous spring, Your fair wind's ministry?
I sinned, and I went solitary from Paradise,
But angels could not people Your world's vacancy;
On my all-venturing nature the naked wilderness
Pours blessings out, that realm You left to anarchy.
A spirit that craves danger is not lured by parks,
Where no close ambush holds a lurking enemy.
The abode of Love lies far beyond Your seraphs' wings;
None find but who desire and dare infinitely.

غزل نمبر ۲

اثر کرے نہ کرے، سن تو لے مری فریاد ۔۔۔ نہیں ہے داد کا طالب یہ بندۂ آزاد!

یہ مُشتِ خاک، یہ صرصر، یہ وسعتِ افلاک ۔۔۔ کرم ہے یا کہ ستم تیری لذتِ ایجاد!

ٹھہر سکا نہ ہوائے چمن میں نیمۂ گل! ۔۔۔ یہی ہے فصلِ بہاری؟ یہی ہے بادِ مراد؟

قصوروار، غریب الدّیار ہوں لیکن ۔۔۔ ترا خرابہ فرشتے نہ کرسکے آباد!

مری جفا طلبی کو دعائیں دیتا ہے ۔۔۔ وہ دشتِ سادہ، وہ تیرا جہانِ بے بنیاد!

خطر پسند طبیعت کو سازگار نہیں ۔۔۔ وہ گلستاں کہ جہاں گھات میں نہ ہو صیّاد!

مقامِ شوق ترے قدسیوں کے بس کا نہیں

انھیں کا کام ہے یہ جن کے حوصلے ہیں زیاد!

21. Ghazal No. 3

CONTRARY runs our planet, the stars whirl fast, oh Saqi!
In every atom's heartbeat a Doomsday blast, oh Saqi!
Torn from God's congregation its dower of faith and reason,
And godlessness in fatal allurement dressed, oh Saqi!
For our inveterate sickness, our wavering heart, the cure—
That same joy-dropping nectar as in the past, oh Saqi.
Within Islam's cold temple no fire of longing stirs,
For still your face is hidden, veiled and unguessed, oh Saqi.
Unchanged is Persia's garden: soil, stream, Tabriz, unchanged;
And yet with no new Rumi is her land graced, oh Saqi.
But of his barren acres Iqbal will not despair:
A little rain, and harvests shall wave at last, oh Saqi!
On me, a beggar, secrets of empire are bestowed;
My songs are worth the treasures Parvez amassed, oh Saqi.

غزل نمبر ۳

دگرگوں ہے جہاں، تاروں کی گردِش تیز ہے ساقی! دلِ ہر ذرّہ میں غوغائے رستا خیز ہے ساقی!

متاعِ دین و دانش لُٹ گئی اللہ والوں کی یہ کس کافر ادا کا غمزۂ خوں ریز ہے ساقی!

وہی دیرینہ بیماری، وہی نامحکمی دل کی! علاج اس کا وہی آبِ نشاط انگیز ہے ساقی!

حرم کے دل میں سوزِ آرزو پیدا نہیں ہوتا! کہ پیدائی تری اب تک حجاب آمیز ہے ساقی!

نہ اُٹھا پھر کوئی رومی عجم کے لالہ زاروں سے وہی آب و گلِ ایراں، وہی تبریز ہے ساقی!

نہیں ہے ناامید اقبال اپنی کشتِ ویراں سے ذرا نم ہو تو یہ مٹی بہت زرخیز ہے ساقی!

فقیرِ راہ کو بخشے گئے اسرارِ سلطانی

بہا میری نوا کی دولتِ پرویز ہے ساقی

22. Ghazal No. 4

SET out once more that cup, that wine, oh Saqi—
Let my true place at last be mine, oh Saqi!
Three centuries India's wineshops have been closed,
And now for your largesse we pine, oh Saqi;
My flask of poetry held the last few drops—
Unlawful, says our crabb'd divine, oh Saqi.
Truth's forest hides no lion-hearts now: men grovel
Before the priest, or the saint's shrine, oh Saqi.
Who has borne off Love's valiant sword? About
An empty scabbard Wisdom's hands twine, oh Saqi.
Verse lights up life, while hearts burn bright, but fades
For ever when those rays decline, oh Saqi.
Bereave not of its moon my night; I see
A full moon in your goblet shine, oh Saqi!

غزل نمبر ۴

ہاتھ آ جائے مجھے میرا مقام اے ساقی!	لا پھر اک بار وہی بادہ و جام اے ساقی!
اب مناسب ہے ترا فیض ہو عام اے ساقی!	تین سو سال سے ہیں ہند کے میخانے بند
شیخ کہتا ہے کہ ہے یہ بھی حرام اے ساقی!	مری مینائے غزل میں تھی ذرا سی باقی
رہ گئے صوفی و ملّا کے غلام اے ساقی!	شیر مردوں سے ہوا پیشۂ تحقیق تھی
علم کے ہاتھ میں خالی ہے نیام اے ساقی!	عشق کی تیغِ جگردار اڑالی کس نے؟
ہو نہ روشن، تو سخن مرگِ دوام اے ساقی!	سینہ روشن ہو تو ہے سوزِ سخن عین حیات
ترے پیمانے میں ہے ماہِ تمام اے ساقی!	تو مری رات کو مہتاب سے محروم نہ رکھ

23. *Ghazal No. 5*

SLOW fire of longing—wealth beyond compare;
I would not change my prayer-mat for Heaven's chair!

Ill fits this world Your freemen, ill the next:
Death's hard yoke frets them here, life's hard yoke there.

Close veils inflame the loiterer in Love's lane;
Your long reluctance fans my passion's flare.

The hawk lives out his days in rock and desert,
Tame nest-twig-carrying his proud claws forswear.

Was it book-lesson, or father's glance, that taught
The son of Abraham what a son should bear?

Bold hearts, firm souls, come pilgrim to my tomb;
I taught poor dust to tower hill-high in air.

Truth has no need of me for tiring-maid;
To stain the tulip red is Nature's care.

غزل نمبر ۵

متاعِ بے بہا ہے درودسوزِ آرزو مندی
مقام بندگی دے کر نہ لوں شانِ خداوندی

ترے آزاد بندوں کی نہ یہ دنیا، نہ وہ دنیا
یہاں مرنے کی پابندی، وہاں جینے کی پابندی

حجاب اکسیر ہے آوارۂ کوئے محبت کو
مری آتش کو بھڑکاتی ہے تیری دیر پیوندی

گزر اوقات کرلیتا ہے یہ کوہ و بیاباں میں
کہ شاہیں کے لیے ذلت ہے کارِ آشیاں بندی!

یہ فیضانِ نظر تھا یا کہ مکتب کی کرامت تھی
سکھائے کس نے اسمٰعیلؑ کو آدابِ فرزندی؟

زیارت گاہِ اہلِ عزم و ہمت ہے لحد میری
کہ خاک راہ کو میں نے بتایا رازِ الوندی!

مری مشّاطگی کی کیا ضرورت حسنِ معنی کو
کہ فطرت خود بخود کرتی ہے لالے کی حنابندی!

24. *Ghazal No. 6*

HAVE you forgotten then my heart of old,
That college of Love, that whip that bright eyes hold?

The school-bred demi-goddesses of this age
Lack the carved grace of the old pagan mould!

This is a strange world, neither cage nor nest,
With no calm nook in all its spacious fold.

The vine awaits your bounteous rain: no more
Is the Magian wine in Persia's taverns sold.

My comrades thought my songs were of Spring's kindling—
How should they know what in Love's notes is told?

Out of my flesh and blood you made this earth;
Its quenchless fever the martyr's crown of gold.

My days supported by your alms, I do not
Complain against my friends, or the times scold.

غزل نمبر ۲

تجھے یاد کیا نہیں ہے مرے دل کا وہ زمانہ؟ ۔۔۔ وہ ادب گہِ محبت! وہ نگہ کا تازیانہ!

یہ بتانِ عصرِ حاضر کہ بنے ہیں مدرسے میں ۔۔۔ نہ ادائے کافرانہ! نہ تراشِ آزرانہ!

نہیں اس کھلی فضا میں کوئی گوشنۂ فراغت ۔۔۔ یہ جہاں عجب جہاں ہے، نہ قفس، نہ آشیانہ!

رگِ تاک منتظر ہے تری بارشِ کرم کی ۔۔۔ کہ عجم کے میکدوں میں نہ رہی ئے مغانہ!

مرے ہم صفیر اسے بھی اثرِ بہار سمجھے! ۔۔۔ انھیں کیا خبر کہ کیا ہے یہ نوائے عاشقانہ!

مرے خاک و خوں سے تو نے یہ جہاں کیا ہے پیدا ۔۔۔ صلۂ شہید کیا ہے؟ تب و تابِ جاودانہ!

تری بندہ پروری سے مرے دن گزر رہے ہیں ۔۔۔ نہ گلہ ہے دوستوں کا، نہ شکایتِ زمانہ!

25. *Ghazal No. 7*

LOVELY, oh Lord, this fleeting world; but why
Must the frank heart, the quick brain, droop and sigh?
Though usury mingle somewhat with his godship,

The white man is the world's arch-diety;
His asses graze in fields of rose and poppy:
One wisp of hay to genius You deny;
His Church abounds with roasts and ruby wines:
Sermons and saws are all Your mosques supply.
Your laws are just, but their expositors
Bedevil the Quran, twist it awry;
Your paradise no-one has seen: in Europe
No village but with paradise can vie.
—Long, long have my thoughts wandered about heaven;
Now in the moon's blind caverns let them stay!
I, dowered by Nature with empyreal essence,
Am dust—but not through dust does my way lie;
Not East nor West my home, nor Samarkand,
Nor Ispahan nor Delhi; in ecstasy,
God-filled, I roam, speaking what truth I see—
No fool for priests, nor yet of this age's fry.
My folk berate me, the stranger does not love me:
Hemlock for sherbet I could never cry;
How could a weigher of truth see Mount Damavand
And think a common refuse-heap as high?
In Nimrod's fire faith's silent witness, not
Like mustard-seed in the grate, burned splutteringly,—
Blood warm, gaze keen, right-following, wrong-forswearing,
In fetters free, prosperous in penury,
In fair or foul untamed and light of heart—
Who can steal laughter from a flower's bright eye?

—Will no-one hush this too proud thing Iqbal
Whose tongue God's presence-chamber could not tie!

غزل نمبر ۷

یارب! یہ جہانِ گزراں خوب ہے لیکن
کیوں خوار ہیں مردانِ صفاکیش و ہنرمند؟

گو اس کی خدائی میں مہاجن کا بھی ہے ہاتھ
دنیا تو سمجھتی ہے فرنگی کو خداوند!

تو برگِ گیا ہے نہ دہی اہلِ خرد را
او کشتِ گل و لالہ بہ نجشد بہ خرے چند!

حاضر ہیں کلیسا میں کباب و نئے گلگوں
مسجد میں دھرا کیا ہے بجز مؤعظہ و پند!

احکام ترے حق ہیں، مگر اپنے مقسر
تاویل سے قرآں کو بنا سکتے ہیں پازند!

فردوس جو تیرا ہے، کسی نے نہیں دیکھا
افرنگ کا ہر قریہ ہے فردوس کی ماند!

مدت سے ہے آوارۂ افلاک مرا فکر
کردے اسے اب چاند کی غاروں میں نظر بند!

فطرت نے مجھے بخشے ہیں جوہر ملکوتی!
خاکی ہوں مگر خاک سے رکھتا نہیں پیوند!

درویش خد مست نہ شرقی ہے، نہ غربی
گھر میرا نہ دلّی، نہ صفاہاں، نہ سمرقند!

کہتا ہوں وہی بات سمجھتا ہوں جسے حق
نے ابلہ مسجد ہوں، نہ تہذیب کا فرزند!

اپنے بھی خفا مجھ سے ہیں، بیگانے بھی ناخوش
میں زہر ہلاہل کو کبھی کہہ نہ سکا قند!

مشکل ہے کہ اک بندۂ حق بین و حق اندیش
خاشاک کے تودے کو کہے کوہ دماوند!

ہوں آتشِ نمرود کے شعلوں میں بھی خاموش
میں بندۂ مومن ہوں، نہیں دانہ اسپند!

پُرسوز و نظر بازو نکوبیں و کم آزاد
آزاد و گرفتار و تہی کیسہ و خورسند!

ہر حال میں میرا دل بے قید ہے خرّم
کیا چھینے گا غنچے سے کوئی ذوقِ شکر خند!

چپ رہ نہ سکا نہ سکا حضرتِ یزداں میں بھی اقبالؔ
کرتا کوئی اس بندۂ گستاخ کا منہ بند!

26. Ghazal No. 8

ALL Nature's vastness cannot contain you, oh
My madness: vain, those wanderings to and fro
In deserts! By Selfhood only are the spells
Of sense broken,—that power we did not know.
Rub your eyes, sluggard! Light is Nature's law,
And not unknown to Ocean its waves flow.
Where reason and revelation war, faith errs
To think the Mystic on his cross its foe,
For God's pure souls, in thraldom or on thrones,
Have one safe shield, his scorn of this world's show.
But do not, Gabriel, envy my rapture: better
For Heaven's douce folk the prayer and the beads' neat row!

I have seen many a wineshop East and West;
But here no Saqi, there in the grape no glow.
In Iran no more, in Tartary no more,
Those world-renouncers who could overthrow

غزل نمبر ۸

سما سکتا نہیں پہنائے فطرت میں مراسودا
غلط تھا اے جنوں شاید ترا اندازۂ صحرا!
خودی سے اس طلسمِ رنگ و بو کو توڑ سکتے ہیں
یہی توحید تھی جس کو نہ تو سمجھا نہ میں سمجھا
نگہ پیدا کر اے غافل تجلّی عینِ فطرت ہے
کہ اپنی موج سے بیگانہ رہ سکتا نہیں دریا
رقابت علم و عرفاں میں غلط بینی ہے منبر کی
کہ وہ حلّاج کی سولی کو سمجھا ہے رقیب اپنا
خدا کے پاک بندوں کو حکومت میں،غلامی میں
زِرہ کوئی اگر محفوظ رکھتی ہے تو استغنا!
نہ کر تقلید اے جبریل میرے جذب و مستی کی
تن آساں عرشیوں کو ذکر و تسبیح و طواف اولٰی!

بہت دیکھے ہیں میں نے مشرق و مغرب کے میخانے
یہاں ساقی نہیں پیدا، وہاں بے ذوق ہے صہبا!
نہ ایراں میں رہے باقی، نہ توراں میں رہے باقی
وہ بندے فقر تھا جن کا ہلاکِ قیصر و کسرٰی

Great kings; the Prophet's heir filches and sells
The blankets of the Prophet's kin. When to
The Lord I was denounced for crying Doomsday
Too soon, by that Archangel who must blow
Its trumpet, God made answer—*Is Doomsday far
When Mecca sleeps while China worship?*—Though
The bowl of faith finds none to pour, the beaker
Of modern thought brims with the wine of No.
Subdued by the dextrous fiddler's chords there murmurs
In the lowest string the wail of Europe's woe—
Her waters that have bred the shark now breed
The storm-wave that will smash its den below!

Slavery—exile from the love of beauty:
Beauty—whatever free men reckon so;
Trust no slave's eyes, clear sight and liberty
Go hand in hand. His own resolves bestow

یہی شیخِ حرم ہے جو چُرا کر بیچ کھاتا ہے
گلیمِ بُوذرؓ و دلقِ اویسؓ و چادرِ زہراؓ!
حضورِ حق میں اسرافیل نے میری شکایت کی
یہ بندہ وقت سے پہلے قیامت کر نہ دے برپا!
ندا آئی کہ آشوبِ قیامت سے یہ کیا کم ہے
'گرفتہ چینیاں احرام و مکی خفتہ دربطحا!'
لبالب شیشۂ تہذیبِ حاضر ہے مۓ لا سے
مگر ساقی کے ہاتھوں میں نہیں پیمانۂ اِلّا
دبا رکھا ہے اس کو زخمہ ور کی تیز دستی نے
بہت نیچے سُروں میں ہے ابھی یورپ کا واویلا
اسی دریا سے اُٹھتی ہے وہ موجِ تند جولاں بھی
نہنگوں کے نشیمن جس سے ہوتے ہیں تہ و بالا
غلامی کیا ہے؟ ذوقِ حسن و زیبائی سے محرومی
جسے زیبا کہیں آزاد بندے، ہے وہی زیبا!
بھروسا کر نہیں سکتے غلاموں کی بصیرت پر
کہ دنیا میں فقط مردانِ حر کی آنکھ ہے بینا!

The empire of To-day on him who fishes
To-morrow's pearl up from Time's undertow.

The Frankish glassblowers' arts can make stone run:
My alchemy makes glass flint-hard. Pharaoh
Plotted and plots against me; but what harm?
Heaven lifts my hand, like Moses', white as snow;
Earth's rubbish-heaps can never quell this spark
God struck to light whole deserts, His flambeau!
Love, self-beholding, self-sustaining, stands
Unawed at the gates of Caesar or Khosro;
If moon or Pleiads fall my prey, what wonder—
Myself bound fast to the Prophet's saddle-bow!
He—Guide, Last Envoy, Lord of All—lent brightness
Of Sinai to our dust; Love's eyes, not slow

To kindle, hail him Alpha and Omega,
Chapter, and Word, and Book.
                                        I would not go
Pearl-diving there, for reverence of Sana'i;
But in these tides a million pearls still grow.

وہی ہے صاحبِ امروز جس نے اپنی ہمت سے

زمانے کے سمندر سے نکالا گوہرِ فردا

فرنگی شیشہ گر کے فن سے پتھر ہوگئے پانی

مری اکسیر نے شیشے کو بخشی سختیٔ خارا!

رہے ہیں، اور ہیں فرعون مری گھات میں اب تک

مگر کیا غم کہ میری آستیں میں ہے یدِبیضا!

وہ چنگاری خس و خاشاک سے کس طرح دب جائے

جسے حق نے کیا ہو نیستاں کے واسطے پیدا

محبت خویشتن بینی، محبت خویشتن داری

محبت آستانِ قیصر و کسریٰ سے بے پروا

عجب کیا گرمہ و پرویں مرے نخچیر ہو جائیں

کہ برفتراکِ صاحب دولتے بستم سرِخودرا'

وہ دانائے سُبل، ختم الرسل، مولائے کل جس نے

غبارِراہ کو بخشا فروغِ وادیٔ سینا

نگاہِ عشق و ہستی میں وہی اوّل، وہی آخر

وہی قرآں، وہی فرقاں، وہی یٰسیں، وہی طہٰ!

سنائی کے ادب سے میں نے غواصی نہ کی ورنہ

ابھی اس بحر میں باقی ہیں لاکھوں لولوئے لالا!

27. Ghazal No. 9

FABRIC of earth and wind and wave!
      Who is the secret, you or I,
Brought into light? or who the dark
      world of what hides yet, you or I?
Here in this night of grief and pain,
      trouble and toil, that men call life,
Who is the dawn, or who dawn's prayer
      cried from the minaret, you or I?
Who is the load that Time and Space
      bear on their shoulder? Who the prize
Run for with fiery feet by swift
      daybreak and sunset, you or I?
You are a pinch of dust and blind,
      I am a pinch of dust that feels;
Through the dry land, Existence, who
      flows like a streamlet, you or I?

غزل نمبر 9

عالمِ آب و خاک و باد! سِرِّ عیاں ہے تو کہ میں؟
وہ جو نظر سے ہے نہاں، اُس کا جہاں ہے تو کہ میں؟

وہ شبِ درد و سوزوغم، کہتے ہیں زندگی جسے
اُس کی سحر ہے تو کہ میں؟ اُس کی اذاں ہے تو کہ میں؟

کس کی نمود کے لیے شام و سحر ہیں گرمِ سیر
شانہٴ روزگار پر بارِگراں ہے تو کہ میں؟

تو کفِ خاک و بے بصر! میں کفِ خاک و خودنگر!
کشتِ وجود کے لیے آبِ رواں ہے تو کہ میں؟

28. Ghazal No. 10

HILL and vale once more under the poppy's lamp are bright,
In my heart the nightingale has set new songs alight;
Violet, violet, azure, azure, golden, golden, mantles—
Flowers, or fairies of the desert, rank on rank in sight?
On the rose-spray dawn's soft breeze has left a pearl of dew,
Now the sunbeam turns this gem a yet more glittering white.
Town or woodland, which is sweeter, if for her unveiling
Careless beauty love towns less than where green woods invite?

Delve into your soul and there seek out life's buried tracks;
Will you not be mine? then be not mine, be your own right!
World of soul—the world of fire and ecstasy and longing:
World of sense—the world of gain that fraud and cunning
    blight;
Treasure of the soul once won is never lost again:
Treasured gold, a shadow—wealth soon comes and soon takes
    flight.

In the spirit's world I have not seen a white man's Raj,
In that world I have not seen Hindu and Muslim fight.
Shame and shame that hermit's saying poured on me—You
    forfeit
Body and soul alike if once you cringe to another's might!

غزل نمبر ۱۰

پھر چراغِ لالہ سے روشن ہوئے کوہ و دمن

پھول ہیں صحرا میں یا پریاں قطار اندر قطار

برگِ گل پر رکھ گئی شبنم کا موتی بادِ صبح

حسنِ بے پروا کو اپنی بے نقابی کے لیے

اپنے من میں ڈوب کر پاجا سراغِ زندگی

من کی دنیا؟ من کی دنیا سوز و مستی، جذب و شوق

من کی دولت ہاتھ آتی ہے تو پھر جاتی نہیں

من کی دنیا میں نہ پایا میں نے افرنگی کا راج

پانی پانی کر گئی مجھ کو قلندر کی یہ بات

تو جھکا جب غیر کے آگے، نہ من تیرا، نہ تن!

مجھ کو پھر نغموں پہ اُکسانے لگا مرغِ چمن

اُودے اُودے، نیلے نیلے، پیلے پیلے پیرہن

اور چمکاتی ہے اس موتی کو سورج کی کرن

ہوں اگر شہروں سے بن پیارے تو شہر اچھے کہ بَن؟

تو اگر میرا نہیں بنتا نہ بن، اپنا تو بن!

تن کی دنیا؟ تن کی دنیا سُود و سودا، مکر و فن

تن کی دولت چھاؤں ہے، آتا ہے دھن، جاتا ہے دھن

من کی دنیا میں نہ دیکھے میں نے شیخ و برہمن

29. Ghazal No. 11

A RECREANT captain, a battle-line thrown back,
The arrow hanging targetless and slack!
Nowhere near you that shell which holds life's pearl;
I have dragged the waves and searched the ocean's track.
Plunge in your Self, on idols dote no more,
Pour out no more heart's blood for paint to deck
Their shrines. I unveil the courts of Love and Death:
Death—life dishonoured; Love—death for honour's sake.

I gleaned in Rumi's company: one bold heart
Is worth of learned heads the whole tame pack;
Once more that voice from Sinai's tree would cry
Fear not! if some new Moses led the attack.
No glitter of Western science could dazzle my eyes
That dust of Medina stains, like collyrium, black.

غزل نمبر ۱۱

میرے سپاہِ نا سزا، لشکریاں شکستہ صف
تیرے محیط میں کہیں گوہرِ زندگی نہیں

عشقِ بتاں سے ہاتھ اُٹھا، اپنی خودی میں ڈوب جا
کھول کے کیا بیاں کروں سرِّ مقامِ مرگ و عشق

صحبتِ پیرِ روم سے مجھ پہ ہوا یہ راز فاش
مثلِ کلیم ہوا گر معرکہ آزما کوئی

خیرہ نہ کر سکا مجھے جلوۂ دانشِ فرنگ

آہ! وہ تیرِ نیم کش جس کا نہ ہو کوئی ہدف
ڈھونڈ چکا میں موجِ موج، دیکھ چکا صدف صدف!

نقش و نگارِ دیر میں خونِ جگر نہ کر تلف!
عشق ہے مرگِ با شرف، مرگِ حیات بے شرف

لاکھ حکیم سر بجیب، ایک کلیم سر بکف
اب بھی درختِ طور سے آتی ہے بانگِ لَاتَخَفْ

سرمہ ہے میری آنکھ کا خاکِ مدینہ و نجف

30. Ghazal No. 12

ALL life is voyaging,
                all things in motion,
Moon, stars, and creatures
                of air and ocean.
To you the champion,
                the lord of battle,
Bright angels offer
                their swords' devotion—
But oh that blindness,
                that craven spirit!
Of your own greatness
                you have no notion.
How long this bondage
                to darkness? Choose now:
A prince's sceptre,—
                a hermit's potion.
I know our priesthood,
                how faint in action,
In sermons pouring
                a languid lotion.

غزل نمبر ۱۲

ہر شے مسافر، ہر چیز راہی!‌ کیا چاند تارے، کیا مرغ و ماہی!‌

تو مردِ میداں، تو میر لشکر نوری حضوری تیرے سپاہی!‌

کچھ قدر اپنی تو نے نہ جانی یہ بے سوادی، یہ کم نگاہی!‌

وینائے دُوں کی کب تک غلامی یا راہبی کر، یا پادشاہی!‌

پیرِ حرم کو دیکھا ہے میں نے کردار بے سوز، گفتار واہی!‌

31. *Ghazal No. 13*

EACH atom pants for glory: greed
Of self-fruition earth's whole creed!
Life that thirsts for no flowering—death:
Self-creation—a godlike deed;
Through Self the mustard-seed becomes
A hill: without, the hill a seed.
The stars wander and do not meet,
To all things severance is decreed;
Pale is the moon of night's last hour
No whispered things of friendship speed.
Your own heart is your candle, your
Own self is all the light you need;
You are this world's sole truth, all else
Illusion such as sorceries breed.
—These desert thorns prick many a doubt:
Do not complain if bare feet bleed.

غزل نمبر ۱۳

ہر چیز ہے محوِ خودنمائی!	ہر ذرّہ شہیدِ کبریائی!
بے ذوق نمودِ زندگی، موت	تعمیرِ خودی میں ہے خدائی!
رائی زورِ خودی سے پربت پربت	پربت ضعفِ خودی سے رائی!
تارے آوارہ و کم آمیز	تقدیرِ وجود ہے جدائی!
یہ پچھلے پہر کا زرد رُو چاند	بے راز و نیازِ آشنائی!
تیری قندیل ہے ترا دل	تُو آپ ہے اپنی روشنائی!
اک تو ہے کہ حق ہے اس جہاں میں	باقی ہے نمودِ سیمیائی!
ہیں عقدہ کشا یہ خارِ صحرا	کم کر گلۂ برہنہ پائی!

32. Ghazal No. 14

BEYOND the stars more worlds: Love's grace
Has other trials yet to face—
Not void of life those far-off deeps,
Where thousand caravans run their race;
In other gardens other nests—
Be not content with earth's embrace;
Why for one lost home mourn, when grief
Can find so many a lodging-place?
You are a falcon born to soar,
Still with your wings new heavens keep pace;
Let day-and-night not snare your feet,
Yours are another Time and Space!

Gone, days of crowded solitude;
Now other hearts know my heart's case.

غزل نمبر ۱۴

ابھی عشق کے امتحاں اور بھی ہیں   ستاروں سے آگے جہاں اور بھی ہیں

یہاں سیکڑوں کارواں اور بھی ہیں   تہی زندگی سے نہیں یہ فضائیں

چمن اور بھی آشیاں اور بھی ہیں!   قناعت نہ کر عالمِ رنگ و بُو پر

مقاماتِ آہ و فغاں اور بھی ہیں!   اگر کھو گیا اک نشیمن تو کیا غم

ترے سامنے آسماں اور بھی ہیں   تو شاہیں ہے، پرواز ہے کام تیرا

کہ تیرے زمان و مکاں اور بھی ہیں   اِسی روز و شب میں اُلجھ کر نہ رہ جا

گئے دن کہ تنہا تھا میں انجمن میں

یہاں اب مرے رازداں اور بھی ہیں!

33. *Ghazal No. 15*

ON me no subtle brain though Nature spent,
My dust hides strength to dare the high ascent—
That frantic dust whose eye outranges reason,
Dust by whose madness Gabriel's robe is rent;
That will not creep about its garden gathering
Straw for a nest—unhoused and yet content.
And Allah to this dust a gift of tears
Whose brightness shames the constellations, lent.

غزل نمبر ۱۵

رکھتی ہے مگر طاقتِ پرواز مری خاک!   فطرت نے نہ بخشا مجھے اندیشۂ چالاک

وہ خاک،کہ جبریل کی ہے جس سے قبا چاک!   وہ خاک، کہ ہے جس کا جنوں صیقلِ ادراک

چنتی نہیں پہنائے چمن سے خس و خاشاک!   وہ خاک، کہ پروائے نشیمن نہیں رکھتی

کرتی ہے چمک جن کی ستاروں کوعرق ناک!   اس خاک کو اللہ نے بخشے ہیں وہ آنسو

34. Ghazal No. 16

By men whose eyes see far and wide new cities shall be founded:
Not by old Kufa or Baghdad is my thought's vision bounded!

Rash youth, new-fangled learning, giddy pleasure, gaudy
        plume,—
With these, while these still swarm, the Frankish wineshop is
        surrounded.

Not with philosopher, nor with priest, my business; one lays
        waste
The heart, and one sows discord to keep mind and soul
        confounded;

And for the Phatisee—far from this poor worm be disrespect!
But how to enfranchise Man, is all the problem I have sounded.

The fleshpots of the wealthy are for sale about the world;
Who bears love's toils and pangs earns wealth that God's hand
        has compounded.

I have laid bare such mysteries as the hermit learns, that thought,
In cloister or in college, in true freedom may be grounded.

No fastings of Mahatmas will destroy the Brahmins' sway;
Vainly, when Moses holds no rod, have all his words resounded!

غزل نمبر ۱۶

کریں گے اہلِ نظر تازہ بستیاں آباد
مری نگاہ نہیں سوئے کوفہ و بغداد!

یہ مدرسہ، یہ جواں، یہ سُرور و رعنائی
اِنھیں کے دم سے ہے مَیخانہ فرنگ آباد!

نہ فلسفی سے، نہ مُلّا سے ہے غرض مجھ کو
یہ دل کی موت، وہ اندیشہ و نظر کا فساد!

فقیہہ شہر کی تحقیر! کیا مجال مری
مگر یہ بات کہ مَیں ڈھونڈتا ہوں دل کی کشاد!

خرید سکتے ہیں دنیا میں عشرتِ پرویز
خدا کی دین ہے سرمایۂ غمِ فرہاد!

کیے ہیں فاش رموزِ قلندری مَیں نے
کہ فکرِ مدرسہ و خانقاہ ہو آزاد!

رِشی کے فاقوں سے ٹوٹا نہ برہمن کا طلسم
عصا نہ ہو تو کلیمی ہے کارِ بے بنیاد!

35. *Ghazal No. 17*

STRANGE ways have reason, wit, and intellect,
Sworn foes to faith and feeling in Love's sect;

I know, when subtle quirks ensnare its teachers,
On what sharp reefs my people must be wrecked!
The singing-bird may flutter about my door,
But from her song no notes of mine expect.

Who will tell Turkey this odd rhyme from me
(Since verse the Turks, I hear, do not neglect)—
Why must she think the West her next-door neighbour,
She whom the stars from nearer skies protect!

غزل نمبر ۱۷

شعور و ہوش و خرد کا معاملہ ہے عجیب   مقامِ شوق میں ہیں سب دل و نظر کے رقیب!

میں جانتا ہوں جماعت کا حشر کیا ہوگا   مسائلِ نظری میں اُلجھ گیا ہے خطیب!

اگرچہ میرے نشیمن کا کر رہا ہے طواف   مری نوا میں نہیں طائرِ چمن کا نصیب!

سنا ہے میں نے سخن رس ہے ترکِ عثمانی   سُنائے کون اسے اقبالؔ کا یہ شعرِ غریب!

سمجھ رہے ہیں وہ یورپ کو ہم جوار اپنا

ستارے جن کے نشیمن سے ہیں زیادہ قریب!

36. Six Ruba'iyat

(1)

THY world the fish's and the winged thing's bower;
My world a crying of the sunrise hour;
In Thy world I am helpless and a slave;
In my world is Thy kingdom and Thy power.

(2)

Faith is like Abraham at the stake: to be
Self-honouring and God-drunk, is faith. Hear me,
You whom this age's ways so captivate!
To have no faith is worse than slavery.

(3)

Music of strange lands with Islam's fire blends,
On which the nations' harmony depends;
Empty of concord is the soul of Europe,
Whose civilization to no Mecca bends.

(4)

There's breath in you, but no heart's palpitation—
That breath no eager circle's inspiration.
Go beyond Reason's light: her's is the lamp
That shows the road, not marks the destination.

(5)

Litter- nor camel-faring, I—
Guidepost, no home ensnaring, I—
To burn all dross, my destiny—
Lightning, no harvest-bearing, I!

(6)

Love's madness has departed: in
The Muslim's veins the blood runs thin;
Ranks broken, hearts perplexed, prayers cold,
No feeling deeper than the skin.

چھ رُباعیات

(۱)

تری دنیا جہانِ مُرغ و ماہی مری دنیا فغانِ صبحگاہی

تری دنیا میں مَیں محکوم و مجبور مری دنیا میں تیری پادشاہی!

(۲)

یقیں، مثلِ خلیلؑ آتش نشینی یقیں، اللہ مستی، خود گُزینی

سن، اے تہذیبِ حاضر کے گرفتار غلامی سے بتر ہے بے یقینی!

(۳)

عرب کے سوز میں سازِ عجم ہے حرم کا رازِ توحیدِ اُمم ہے

تہی وحدت سے ہے اندیشۂ غرب کہ تہذیبِ فرنگی بے حرم ہے

(۴)

ترے سینے میں دم ہے، دل نہیں ہے ترا دم گرمیٔ محفل نہیں ہے

گزر جا عقل سے آگے کہ یہ نُور چراغِ راہ ہے، منزل نہیں ہے

(۵)

سوارِ ناقہ و محمل نہیں مَیں نشانِ جادہ ہوں، منزل نہیں مَیں

مری تقدیر ہے خاشاک سوزی فقط بجلی ہوں میں، حاصل نہیں مَیں

(۶)

محبت کا جنوں باقی نہیں ہے مسلمانوں میں خوں باقی نہیں ہے

صفیں کج، دل پریشاں، سجدہ بے ذوق کہ جذبِ اندروں باقی نہیں ہے

37. The Mosque of Cordoba

DAY succeeding to night—moulder of all time's works!
Day succeeding to night—fountain of life and of death!
Chain of the days and nights—two-coloured thread of silk
Woven by Him that is, into His being's robe!

What other sense have your nights, what have your days, but
      one
Long blank current of time empty of sunset or dawn?
All Art's wonders arise only to vanish once more;
All things built on this earth sink as if built on sand!
Inward and outward things, first things and last, must die;
Things from of old or new-born find their last goal in death.

Yet, in this frame of things, gleams of immortal life
Show where some servant of God wrought into some high
      shape

Chain of the days and nights—sigh of eternity's harp,
Height and depth of all things possible, God-revealed.
You are brought to their test; I am brought to their test—
Day revolving with night, touchstone of all this world;
Weighed in their scales you and I, weighed and found
wanting, shall both
Find in death our reward, find in extinction our wage;

مسجدِ قرطبہ

(ہسپانیہ کی سرزمین، بالخصوص قرطبہ میں لکھی گئی)

سلسلۂ روز و شب، نقش گرِ حادثات

سلسلۂ روز و شب، اصلِ حیات و ممات

سلسلۂ روز و شب، تارِ حریرِ دو رنگ

جس سے بناتی ہے ذات اپنی قبائے صفات

تیرے شب و روز کی اور حقیقت ہے کیا

ایک زمانے کی رَو جس میں نہ دن ہے نہ رات!

آنی و فانی تمام معجزہ ہائے ہنر

کارِ جہاں بے ثبات! کارِ جہاں بے ثبات!

اوّل و آخر فنا، باطن و ظاہر فنا

نقشِ کہن ہو کہ نَو، منزلِ آخر فنا

ہے مگر اس نقش میں رنگِ ثباتِ دوام

جس کو کیا ہو کسی مردِ خدا نے تمام

سلسلۂ روز و شب، سازِ ازل کی فغاں

جس سے دکھاتی ہے ذات زیر و بمِ ممکنات

تجھ کو پرکھتا ہے یہ، مجھ کو پرکھتا ہے یہ

سلسلۂ روز و شب، صیرفیِ کائنات

تو ہو اگر کم عیار، میں ہوں اگر کم عیار

موت ہے تیری برات، موت ہے میری برات

Work whose perfection is still bright with the splendour of
      Love—
Love, the well-spring of life; Love, on which death has no
      claim.

Swiftly its tyrannous flood time's long current may roll:
Love itself is a tide, stemming all opposite waves.
Other ages in Love's calendar are set down,
Ages as yet unnamed, far from this now-flowing hour;
Love is Gabriel's breath, Love is Muhammad's strong heart,
Love is the envoy of God, Love the utterance of God.
Even our mortal clay, touched by Love's ecstasy, glows;
Love is a new-pressed wine, Love is the goblet of kings,
Love the priest of the shrine, Love the commander of hosts,
Love the son of the road, counting a thousand homes.
Love's is the plectrum that draws music from live's taut
      strings—
Love's is the warmth of life, Love's is the radiance of life.

Shrine of Cordoba! from Love all your existence is sprung,
Love that can know no end, stranger to Then-and-Now.
Colour or stone and brick, music and song or speech,
Only the heart's warm blood feeds such marvels of craft;

Flint with one drop of that blood turns to a beating heart—
Melody, mirth and joy gush out of warm heart's-blood.

مرد خدا کا عمل عشق سے صاحبِ فروغ
عشق ہے اصلِ حیات، موت ہے اُس پر حرام

تُند و سبک سیر ہے گرچہ زمانے کی رَو
عشق خود اک سیل ہے، سیل کو لیتا ہے تھام

عشق کی تقویم میں عصرِ رواں کے سوا
اور زمانے بھی ہیں جن کا نہیں کوئی نام

عشق دمِ جبریل، عشق دلِ مصطفیؐ
عشق خدا کا رسول، عشق خدا کا کلام

عشق کی مستی سے ہے پیکرِ گُل تابناک
عشق ہے صہبائے خام، عشق ہے کاسُ الکرام

عشق فقیہہِ حرم، عشق امیرِ جُنود
عشق ہے ابن السبیل، اس کے ہزاروں مقام

عشق کے مضراب سے نغمۂ تارِ حیات
عشق سے نورِ حیات، عشق سے نارِ حیات

اے حرمِ قرطبہ! عشق سے تیرا وجود
عشق سراپا دوام، جس میں نہیں رفت و بود

رنگ ہو یا خشت و سنگ، چنگ ہو یا حرف و صَوت
معجزۂ فن کی ہے خونِ جگر سے نمود

قطرۂ خونِ جگر سِل کو بناتا ہے دل
خونِ جگر سے صدا سوز و سُرور و سرود

Yours the soul-quickening pile, mine the soul-kindling verse,
Yours to knock at men's hearts, mine to open their gates.
Not less exalted than high Heaven is the human breast,
Handful of dust though it be, bounded by that blue sky.
What, to Him Who is Light, is it to watch men kneel?
He cannot feel this fire melting our limbs as we pray.
I from the infidel East—see with what fervour I glow,
Blessings on God and His Saint filling my soul and my mouth:
Fervently sounds my voice, ardently sounds my lute,
God is God, like a song, thrilling through every vein!

Outward and inward grace, witness in you for him,
Prove your builder, like you, fair of shape and of soul;
Firm those foundations are fixed, countless those pillars soar
Like an array of palms over the Syrian sands.

Light such as Moses beheld gleams on those walls, that roof,
High on the minaret's top Gabriel sits enthroned!
Never can Muslim despair: he, reciting his creed,
Stands before God where once Moses and Abraham stood.
Limitless is his world, endless horizons are his,
Tigris and Danube and Nile billows that roll in his sea;

تیری فضا دل فروز، میری نوا سینہ سوز

تجھ سے دلوں کا حضور، مجھ سے دلوں کی کشُود

عرشِ معلّٰی سے کم سینۂ آدم نہیں

گرچہ کفِ خاک کی حد ہے سپہرِ کبُود

پیکرِ نوری کو ہے سجدہ میسر تو کیا

اس کو میسر نہیں سوز و گدازِ سجُود

کافرِ ہندی ہوں میں، دیکھ مرا ذوق و شوق

دل میں صلوٰۃ و درود، لب پہ صلوٰۃ و درود

شوق مری لَے میں ہے، شوق مری نَے میں ہے

نغمۂ اللہ ہُو، میرے رگ و پَے میں ہے

تیرا جلال و جمال، مردِ خدا کی دلیل

وہ بھی جلیل و جمیل، تو بھی جلیل و جمیل

تیری بنا پائندار، تیرے ستوں بے شمار

شام کے صحرا میں ہو جیسے ہجومِ نخیل

تیرے دروبام پر وادئ ایمن کا نور

تیرا منارِ بلند جلوہ گہِ جبریل

مٹ نہیں سکتا کبھی مردِ مسلماں کہ ہے

اس کی اذانوں سے فاش سرِّ کلیمؑ و خلیلؑ

اس کی زمیں بے حدود، اس کا اُفق بے ثغُور

اس کے سمندر کی موج، دجلہ و دینیوب و نیل

Fabulous days have been his, strange are the tales he can tell,
He who to ages outworn brought the command to depart;
He who gladdens the gay, rides in the lists of Love,
Pure and unmixed his cup, tempered and pure his steel,
Warrior armed in this mail: *There is no god but God*,
Under the shadow of swords refuged by *no god but God*.

Here stands his inmost self manifest in your stones,
Fire of passionate days, rapture of melting nights;

Here his high station displayed, here his high-mounting thoughts,
Here his joy and desire, self-abasement and pride.

As is the hand of God, so the Believer's hand,
Potent, guided by craft, strong to create and to rule.
Fashioned of dust and of light, creature divine of soul,
Careless of both the worlds beats his not humble heart;
Frugal of earthly hope, splendid of purpose, he earns
Friendship with courteous mien, wins every voice by his glance;
Mild in the social hour, swift in the hour of pursuit,
Whether in feast or in fray pure in conscience and deed.
Round His servant's firm faith God's great compasses turn;
All this universe else shadow, illusion and myth.

اس کے زمانے عجیب، اس کے فسانے غریب

عہدِ کہن کو دیا اس نے پیامِ رحیل

ساقیٔ اربابِ ذوق، فارسِ میدانِ شوق

بادہ ہے اس کا رحیق، تیغ ہے اس کی اصیل

مردِ سپاہی ہے وہ، اس کی زرہ لاالٰہ

سایۂ شمشیر میں اس کی پنہ لاالٰہ

تجھ سے ہوا آشکار بندۂ مومن کا راز

اس کے دنوں کی تپش، اس کی شبوں کا گداز

اس کا مقامِ بلند، اس کا خیالِ عظیم

اس کا سرور اس کا شوق، اس کا نیاز، اس کا ناز

ہاتھ ہے اللہ کا، بندۂ مومن کا ہاتھ

غالب و کار آفریں، کارکشا، کارساز

خاکی و نوری نہاد، بندۂ مولا صفات

ہر دوجہاں سے غنی، اس کا دلِ بے نیاز

اس کی امیدیں قلیل، اس کے مقاصد جلیل

اس کی ادا دل فریب، اس کی نگہ دل نواز

نرم دمِ گفتگو، گرم دمِ جستجو

رزم ہو یا بزم ہو، پاک دل و پاک باز

نقطۂ پرکارِ حق، مردِ خدا کا یقیں

اور یہ عالم تمام وہم و طلسم و مجاز

He is Reason's last goal, he is the harvest of Love,
He in creation's hall sets all spirits ablaze.

Shrine of the lovers of art! Visible power of the Faith!
Sacred as Mecca you made, once, Andalusia's soil.
If there is under these skies loveliness equal to yours,
Only in Muslim hearts, nowhere else can it be.

Ah, those proud cavaliers, champions Arabia sent forth
Pledged to the splendid Way, knights of the truth and the creed!
Through their empire a strange secret was understood:
Friends of mankind hold sway not to command but to serve.
Europe and Asia from them gathered instruction: the West
Lay in darkness, and their wisdom discovered the path.
Even to-day in this land rich with their blood, dwells a race
Carefree, open of heart, simple and smiling-faced;
Even to-day in this land eyes like the soft gazelle's
Dart those glances whose barbs stick in the breast where they
     fall;
Even to-day in its breeze fragrance of Yemen still floats,
Even to-day in its songs echoes live on of Hejaz.
Under the stars your realm lies like a heaven; alas!
Ages are fled since your courts heard their last prayer-call sound.

عقل کی منزل ہے وہ، عشق کا حاصل ہے وہ
حلقۂ آفاق میں گرمیِ محفل ہے وہ

کعبۂ اربابِ فن! سطوتِ دین میں
تجھ سے حرم مرتبت اندلسیوں کی زمیں

ہے تہِ گردوں اگر حُسن میں تیری نظیر
قلبِ مسلماں میں ہے اور نہیں ہے کہیں

آہ وہ مردانِ حق! عربی شہسوار
حاملِ خُلقِ عظیم، صاحبِ صدق و یقیں

جن کی حکومت سے ہے فاش یہ رمزِ غریب
سلطنتِ اہلِ دل فقر ہے، شاہی نہیں

جن کی نگاہوں نے کی تربیتِ شرق و غرب
ظلمتِ یورپ میں تھی جن کی خرد راہ بیں

جن کے لہو کے طفیل آج بھی ہیں اندلسی
خوش دل و گرم اختلاط، سادہ و روشن جبیں

آج بھی اس دیس میں عام ہے چشمِ غزال
اور نگاہوں کے تیر آج بھی ہیں دل نشیں

بوئے یمن آج بھی اس کی ہواؤں میں ہے
رنگِ حجاز آج بھی اس کی نواؤں میں ہے

دیدۂ انجم میں ہے تیری زمیں، آسماں
آہ کہ صدیوں سے ہے تیری فضا بے اذاں

What new halting-place now, what far valley, has Love's
Dauntless caravan reached, treading its stormy road?

Germany saw, long since, Reformation's rough winds
Blotting the old ways out, sweeping away every trace,
Vicars of Christ and their pomp dwindling to lying words,
Reason's fragile bark launched once more on its course;
Under the eyes of France, Revolution long since
Fashioned anew the whole world known to the men of the
    West;
Rome's chief daughter, grown old worshipping ancient things,
Led by desire of Rebirth found, she too, second youth.
Now in the soul of Islam tumults like those are astir,
Working God's secret will: tongue cannot tell what they mean.
Watch! from that ocean-depth—what comes surging at last!
See how those colours change, there in that azure vault!

Drowned in twilight, a cloud hangs over vale and hill,
Heaped by this sunset with red rubies of Badakhshan.
Simple, poignant, a girl singing her peasant song;
Youth is the current that bears lightly the boat of the heart.

کون سی وادی میں ہے، کون سی منزل میں ہے

عشق بلاخیز کا قافلۂ سخت جاں!

دیکھ چکا المّنی، شورشِ اصلاحِ دیں

جس نے نہ چھوڑے کہیں نقشِ کہن کے نشاں

حرفِ غلط بن گئی عصمتِ پیرِ کنشت

اور ہوئی فکر کی کشتیٔ نازک رواں

چشمِ فرانسیس بھی دیکھ چکی انقلاب

جس سے دگرگوں ہوا مغربیوں کا جہاں

ملّتِ رومی نژاد کہنہ پرستی سے پیر

لذتِ تجدیدہ سے وہ بھی ہوئی پھر جواں

روحِ مسلماں میں ہے آج وہی اضطراب

رازِ خدائی ہے یہ، کہہ نہیں سکتی زباں

دیکھیئے اس بحر کی تہ سے اچھلتا ہے کیا

گنبدِ نیلوفری رنگ بدلتا ہے کیا!

وادیٔ کہسار میں غرقِ شفق ہے سحاب

لعلِ بدخشاں کے ڈھیر چھوڑ گیا آفتاب

سادہ و پُرسوز ہے دخترِ دہقاں کا گیت

کشتیٔ دل کے لیے سیل ہے عہدِ شباب

Flowing Guadalquivir! Here on your bank is one
Gazing at things gone by, dreams of another day.
Destiny's curtain till now muffles the world to be,
Yet, already, its dawn stands before me unveiled;
Were I to lift this mask hiding the face of my thoughts,
Europe could never endure songs as burning as mine!
Death, not life, is the life no revolutions stir:
Change, upheaval, the air breathed by the nations' souls;
Keen as a sword that Fate holds in its hand is a folk
Mindful to reckon its deeds, casting their sum in each age.

Warmed by no blood from the heart, all man's creations are
     botched;
Warmed by no blood from the heart, poetry's rapture grows
     faint.

آب روانِ کبیر! تیرے کنارے کوئی

دیکھ رہا ہے کسی اور زمانے کا خواب

عالمِ نو ہے ابھی پردۂ تقدیر میں

میری نگاہوں میں ہے اس کی سحر بے حجاب

پردہ اُٹھادوں اگر چہرۂ افکار سے

لا نہ سکے گا فرنگ میری نواؤں کی تاب

جس میں نہ ہو انقلاب، موت ہے وہ زندگی

روحِ اُمَم کی حیات کشمکشِ انقلاب

صورتِ شمشیر ہے دستِ قضا میں وہ قوم

کرتی ہے جو ہر زماں اپنے عمل کا حساب

نقش ہیں سب ناتمام، خونِ جگر کے بغیر

نغمہ ہے سودائے خام، خونِ جگر کے بغیر

38. Lenin before God

ALL space and all that breathes bear witness; truth
It is indeed; Thou art, and dost remain.
How could I know that God was or was not,
Where Reason's reckonings shifted hour by hour?
The peerer at planets, the counter-up of plants,
Heard nothing there of Nature's infinite music;
To-day I witnessing acknowledge realms
That I once thought the mummery of the Church.
We, manacled in the chains of day and night!
Thou, moulder of all time's atoms, builder of aeons!
Let me have leave to ask this question, one
Not answered by the subtleties of the schools,

That while I lived under the sky-tent's roof
Like a thorn rankled in my heart, and made
Such chaos in my soul of all its thoughts
I could not keep my tumbling words in bounds.
Oh, of what mortal race art Thou the God?
Those creatures formed of dust beneath these heavens?
Europe's pale cheeks are Asia's pantheon,
And Europe's pantheon her glittering metals.
A blaze of art and science lights the West

لینن

(خدا کے حضور میں)

اے انفس و آفاق میں پیدا ترے آیات

حق یہ ہے کہ ہے زندہ و پائندہ تری ذات

میں کیسے سمجھتا کہ تُو ہے یا کہ نہیں ہے

ہر دم متغیّر تھے خرد کے نظریات

محرم نہیں فطرت کے سرودِ ازلی سے

بینائے کواکب ہو کہ دانائے نباتات!

آج آنکھ نے دیکھا تو وہ عالم ہوا ثابت!

میں جس کو سمجھتا تھا کلیسا کے خرافات

ہم بندِ شب و روز میں جکڑے ہوئے بندے

تو خالق اعصار و نگارندۂ آنات!

اک بات اگر مجھ کو اجازت ہو تو پوچھوں

حل کر نہ سکے جس کو حکیموں کے مقالات

جب تک میں جیا خیمۂ افلاک کے نیچے

کانٹے کی طرح دل میں کھٹکتی رہی یہ بات

گفتار کے اسلوب پہ قابو نہیں رہتا

جب روح کے اندر متلاطم ہوں خیالات

وہ کون سا آدم ہے کہ تُو جس کا ہے معبُود؟

وہ آدمِ خاکی کہ جو ہے زیرِ سماوات؟

مشرق کے خداوند سفیدانِ فرنگی!

مغرب کے خداوند درخشندہ فلِزّات!

یورپ میں بہت روشنیٔ علم و ہنر ہے

With darkness that no Fountain of Life dispels;
In high-reared grace, in glory and in grandeur,
The towering Bank out-tops the cathedral roof;
What they call commerce is a game of dice:
For one, profit, for millions swooping death.
There science, philosophy, scholarship, government,
Preach man's equality and drink men's blood;
Naked debauch, and want, and unemployment—
Are these mean triumphs of the Frankish arts!
Denied celestial grace a nation goes
No further than electricity or steam;
Death to the heart, machines stand sovereign,
Engines that crush all sense of human kindness.
—Yet signs are counted here and there that Fate,
The chessplayer, has check-mated all their cunning.
The Tavern shakes, its warped foundations crack,
The Old Men of Europe sit there numb with fear;
What twilight flush is left those faces now
Is paint and powder, or lent by flask and cup.
Omnipotent, righteous, Thou; but bitter the hours,
Bitter the labourer's chained hours in Thy world!
When shall this galley of gold's dominion founder?
Thy world Thy day of wrath, Lord, stands and waits.

حق یہ ہے کہ بے چشمۂ حیواں ہے یہ ظلمات

رعنائی تعمیر میں، رونق میں، صفا میں

گرجوں سے کہیں بڑھ کے ہیں بنکوں کی عمارات

ظاہر میں تجارت ہے، حقیقت میں جوا ہے

سُود ایک کا لاکھوں کے لیے مرگِ مفاجات

یہ علم، یہ حکمت، یہ تدبّر، یہ حکومت

پیتے ہیں لہو، دیتے ہیں تعلیمِ مساوات

بے کاری و عریانی و مے خواری و افلاس

کیا کم ہیں فرنگی مدنیت کے فتوحات

وہ قوم کہ فیضانِ سماوی سے ہو محروم

حد اُس کے کمالات کی ہے برق و بخارات

ہے دل کے لیے موت مشینوں کی حکومت

احساسِ مروّت کو کچل دیتے ہیں آلات

آثار تو کچھ کچھ نظر آتے ہیں کہ آخر

تدبیر کو تقدیر کے شاطر نے کیا مات

میخانے کی بنیاد میں آیا ہے تزَلزُل

بیٹھے ہیں اسی فکر میں پیرانِ خرابات

چہروں پہ جو سرخی نظر آتی ہے سرِشام

یا غازہ ہے یا ساغر و مینا کی کرامات

تو قادر و عادل ہے مگر تیرے جہاں میں

ہیں تلخ بہت بندۂ مزدور کے اوقات

کب ڈوبے گا سرمایہ پرستی کا سفینہ؟

دنیا ہے تری منتظر روزِ مکافات!

39. God's Command to His Angels

RISE, and from their slumber wake the poor ones of My world!
Shake the walls and windows of the mansions of the great!
Kindle with the fire of faith the slow blood of the slaves!
Make the fearful sparrow bold to meet the falcon's hate!
Close the hour approaches of the kingdom of the poor—
Every imprint of the past find and annihilate!
Find the field whose harvest is no peasant's daily bread—
Garner in the furnace every ripening ear of wheat!
Banish from the house of God the mumbling priest whose
      prayers
Like a veil creation from Creator separate!
God by man's prostrations, by man's vows are idols cheated—
Quench at once in My shrine and their fane the sacred light!
Rear for me another temple, build its walls with mud—
Wearied of their columned marbles, sickened is My sight!
All their fine new world a workshop filled with brittle glass—
Go! My poet of the East to madness dedicate.

فرمانِ خدا

(فرشتوں سے)

اُٹھو! مری دنیا کے غریبوں کو جگا دو   کاخِ اُمرا کے درو دیوار ہلا دو

گرماؤ غلاموں کا لہو سوزِ یقیں سے   کنجشکِ فرومایہ کو شاہیں سے لڑا دو

سلطانیِ جمہور کا آتا ہے زمانہ   جو نقشِ کہن تم کو نظر آئے، مٹا دو

جس کھیت سے دہقاں کو میسر نہیں روزی   اُس کھیت کے ہر خوشۂ گندم کو جلا دو

کیوں خالق و مخلوق میں حائل رہیں پردے   پیرانِ کلیسا کو کلیسا سے اُٹھا دو

حق را بسجودے، صنماں را بطوافے   بہتر ہے چراغِ حرم و دیر بجھا دو

میں ناخوش و بیزار ہوں مرمر کی سِلوں سے   میرے لیے مٹی کا حرم اور بنا دو

تہذیبِ نوی کارِ گہِ شیشہ گراں ہے   آدابِ جنوں شاعرِ مشرق کو سکھا دو!

40. Heaven and the Priest

BEING present myself, my impetuous tongue
    To silence I could not resign
When an order from God of admission on high
    Came the way of that reverend divine;
I humbly addressed the Almighty: Oh Lord,
    Excuse this presumption of mine,
But he'll never relish the virgins of heaven,
    The garden's green borders, the wine!
For Paradise isn't the place for a preacher
    To meddle and muddle and mangle,
And he, pious man—second nature to him
    Is the need to dispute and to jangle;
His business has been to set folk by the ears
    And get nations and sects in a tangle:
Up there in the sky is no Mosque and no Church
    And no Temple—with whom will be wrangle?

مُلّا اور بہشت

میں بھی حاضر تھا وہاں، ضبطِ سخن کر نہ سکا

حق سے جب حضرتِ مُلّا کو ملا حکمِ بہشت

عرض کی میں نے، الٰہی! مری تقصیر معاف

خوش نہ آئیں گے اسے حور و شراب و لبِ کشت!

نہیں فردوس مقامِ جدل و قال و اقوال!

بحث و تکرار اس اللہ کے بندے کی سرشت!

ہے بدآموزیِ اقوام و مِلل کام اس کا

اور جنت میں نہ مسجد، نہ کلیسا، نہ کُنِشت!

41. The Earth is God's

Who rears the seed in the darkness of the ground?
Who lifts the cloud up from the ocean wave?

Who drew here from the west the fruitful wind?
Who made this soil, or who that light of the sun?
Who filled with pearls of grain the tasselled wheat?
Who taught the months by instinct to revolve?

Landlord! this earth is not thine, is not thine,
Nor yet thy fathers'; no, not thine, nor mine.

اَلاَرضُ لِلّٰه!

پالتا ہے بیج کو مٹی کی تاریکی میں کون؟

کون دریاؤں کی موجوں سے اُٹھاتا ہے سحاب؟

کون لایا کھینچ کر پچھّم سے بادِ سازگار؟

خاک یہ کس کی ہے؟ کس کا ہے یہ نورِ آفتاب؟

کس نے بھردی موتیوں سے خوشۂ گندم کی جیب؟

موسموں کو کس نے سکھلائی ہے خوئے انقلاب؟

دِہ خدایا! یہ زمیں تیری نہیں، تیری نہیں!

تیرے آبا کی نہیں، تیری نہیں، میری نہیں!

42. Counsel

An eagle full of years to a young hawk said—
Easy your royal wings through high heaven spread:
To burn in the fire of our own veins is youth!
Strive, and in strife make honey of life's gall;
Maybe the blood of the pigeon you destroy,
My son, is not what makes your swooping joy!

نصیحت

بچۂ شاہیں سے کہتا تھا عقابِ سالخورد
اے ترے شہپر پہ آساں رفعتِ چرخِ بریں!
ہے شباب اپنے لہو کی آگ میں جلنے کا نام
سخت کوشی سے ہے تلخِ زندگانی انگبیں!
جو کبوتر پر جھپٹنے میں مزا ہے اے پسر!
وہ مزا شاید کبوتر کے لہو میں بھی نہیں

43. Poppy of the Wilderness

Oh blue sky-dome, oh world companionless!
Fear comes on me in this wide desolation.
Lost travellers, you and I; what destination
Is yours, bright poppy of the wilderness?

No Prophet walks these hills, or we might be
Twin Sinai-flames; you bloom on Heaven's spray
For the same cause I tore myself away:
To unfold, to be our selves, our wills agree.

On the diver of Love's pearl-bank be God's hand—
In every ocean-drop all ocean's deeps!

The whirlpool mourning for its lost wave weeps,
Born of the sea and never to reach the land.

Man's hot blood makes earth's fevered pulses race,
With stars and sun for audience. Oh cool air
Of the desert! let it be mine too to share
In silence and heart-glow, rapture and grace.

لالۂ صحرا

یہ گنبدِ مینائی، یہ عالمِ تنہائی!

مجھ کو تو ڈراتی ہے اس دشت کی پہنائی!

بھٹکا ہوا راہی میں، بھٹکا ہوا راہی تُو!

منزل ہے کہاں تیری اے لالۂ صحرائی؟

خالی ہے کلیموں سے یہ کوہ و کمر ورنہ

تُو شعلۂ سینائی، میں شعلۂ سینائی!

تُو شاخ سے کیوں پھُوٹا، میں شاخ سے کیوں ٹوٹا

اک جذبۂ پیدائی، اک لذّتِ یکتائی!

غوّاصِ محبت کا اللہ نگہباں ہو

ہر قطرۂ دریا میں، دریا کی ہے گہرائی!

اُس موج کے ماتم میں روتی ہے بھنور کی آنکھ

دریا سے اُٹھی، لیکن ساحل سے نہ ٹکرائی!

ہے گرمیِ آدم سے ہنگامۂ عالم گرم   سورج بھی تماشائی، تارے بھی تماشائی!

اے بادِ بیابانی! مجھ کو بھی عنایت ہو   خاموشی و دل سوزی، سرمستی و رعنائی!

44. To the Saqi

THE caravan of Spring has pitched
Its tents; these hillsides are bewitched—
Lily, narcissus and rose have come,
And the poppy from age-old martyrdom
Red-shrouded, with colours to hide earth's face;
Through rock itself hot pulses race;
Blue, blue the skies, with calm winds blest,
No winged thing loiters in its nest.
Down from the heights that rill comes leaping,
Slipping, spurting, recoiling, creeping,
Stumbling, recovering, while it winds
Through a hundred turnings until it finds
Its way, gnawing through boulders that block
Its channel, through mountain-hearts of rock!
Oh Saqi fair as the poppy, see
How it sings life's message! Pour for me
—Rose-harvest is not every day!—
A fiery wine to purge away
All veils, wine to paint life's soul bright:
That wine, the uttermost worlds' delight,
That holds the eternal rapture, betrays
The eternal secret:—oh Saqi, raise

That secret's curtain, and let this weak
Sparrow challenge the falcon's beak!

ساقی نامہ

ہوا خیمہ زن کاروانِ بہار	اِرم بن گیا دامنِ کوہسار
گل و نرگس و سوسن و نسترن	شہیدِ ازل لالہ خونیں کفن
جہاں چھپ گیا پردۂ رنگ میں	لہو کی ہے گردش رگِ سنگ میں
فضا نیلی نیلی، ہوا میں سرور	ٹھہرتے نہیں آشیاں میں طیُور
وہ جوئے کہستاں اُچکتی ہوئی	اٹکتی، لچکتی، سرکتی ہوئی
اُچھلتی، پھسلتی، سنبھلتی ہوئی	بڑے پیچ کھا کر نکلتی ہوئی
رُکے جب تو سِل چیر دیتی ہے یہ	پہاڑوں کے دل چیر دیتی ہے یہ
ذرا دیکھ اے ساقیٔ لالہ فام!	سُناتی ہے یہ زندگی کا پیام
پلادے مجھے وہ مَے پردہ سوز	کہ آتی نہیں فصلِ گل روز روز
وہ مَے جس سے روشن ضمیرِ حیات	وہ مَے جس سے ہے مستیٔ کائنات
وہ مَے جس میں ہے سوزوسازِ ازل	وہ مَے جس سے کھلتا ہے رازِ ازل

اُٹھا ساقیا پردہ اس راز سے

لڑا دے ممولے کو شہباز سے

The fashions of the age turn round,
From new-tuned strings new harmonies sound;
The Frankish wiles have so leaked out
The Frankish mystagogue halts in doubt,
The hoary arts of politics sink,
In earth's nostrils King and Sultan stink,
The cycle of capitalism is done,
The juggler has shown his tricks and gone.
China starts up from her long dream,
Himalayan fountains boil and steam;
Faran's peak cloven, and Sinai's height—
Moses once more awaits Heaven's light!
But the Muslim who shouts *One God*, at heart
Still wears the sacred thread, his art,
Philosophy, law, divinity
Still tainted with idolatry,
Truth buried in rubbish, a ritual maze
Burying the creed; the preacher's phrase
May charm the ear, but all is bare
Of Love's true fervour: every hair
With syllogistic niceness split
And ravelled with metaphysic wit.
The Sufi, God's knight-errant fearless,
In love unrivalled, in virtue peerless,
Turned sophist roams his inner stage,
Imaginary pilgrimage.
Quenched is devotion's burning spark,
Islam an ash-heap cold and dark.

Again, oh Saqi, the old wine pour,
Let the same cup go round once more;
Lend me Love's wing to soar on, take
My dust and a wheeling firefly make!

زمانے کے انداز بدلے گئے نیا راگ ہے، ساز بدلے گئے

ہوا اس طرح فاش رازِ فرنگ کہ حیرت میں ہے شیشہ بازِ فرنگ

پرانی سیاست گری خوار ہے زمیں میر و سلطاں سے بیزار ہے

گیا دورِ سرمایہ داری گیا تماشا دکھا کر مداری گیا

گراں خواب چینی سنبھلے لگے ہمالہ کے چشمے اُبلنے لگے

دلِ طورِ سینا و فاراں دو نیم تجلّی کا پھر منتظر ہے کلیّم

مسلماں ہے توحید میں گرم جوش مگر دل ابھی تک ہے زنّار پوش

تمدن، تصوف، شریعت، کلام بتانِ عجم کے پجاری تمام!

حقیقت خرافات میں کھو گئی یہ اُمت روایات میں کھو گئی

لبھاتا ہے دل کو کلامِ خطیب مگر لذتِ شوق سے بے نصیب!

بیاں اس کا منطق سے سلجھا ہوا لغت کے بکھیڑوں میں اُلجھا ہوا

وہ صوفی کہ تھا خدمتِ حق میں مرد محبت میں یکتا، حمیت میں فرد

عجم کے خیالات میں کھو گیا یہ سالک مقامات میں کھو گیا

بجھی عشق کی آگ، اندھیر ہے

مسلماں نہیں، راکھ کا ڈھیر ہے

شرابِ کہن پھر پلا ساقیا وہی جام گردش میں لا ساقیا!

مجھے عشق کے پر لگا کر اُڑا مری خاک جگنو بنا کر اُڑا

Set all our minds free, far from reach
Of slavery; let age learn, youth teach;
Your sap keeps green the nation's bough,
Your spirit is its lungs' breath: endow
Our souls with power to throb and feel,
With Ali's passion and Siddiq's zeal!
Pierce us again with your keen darts,
Wake the old longings in our hearts!
So may Fate friend your stars, and those
On earth whose eyes night cannot close
From prayer,—set all young veins afire
With vision like mine, and my desire!
Safe through the whirlpool bring my boat,
But set it, if ever it sticks, afloat!
Death's and life's mysteries tell me, you
To whom the universe stands in view!
These streaming eyes sleep woos in vain,
These fevers smouldering in my brain,
This midnight grief and my head bowed,
These tears, alone or amid the crowd,
These throbbings, these long hauntings, these
Far-questing hopes and auguries,
My nature, creation's looking-glass,
Park through which like gazelles thoughts pass,
My heart, life's battleground, where eager
Armies of doubt break on faith's leaguer:—
These the world-scorner's wealth by which
I, Saqi! scorning the world am rich.

Upon my pilgrim people shower,
Oh shower such treasure, its true dower!

☆ ☆ ☆

خرد کو غلامی سے آزاد کر   جوانوں کو پیروں کا استاد کر

ہری شاخِ ملّت ترے نم سے ہے   نفس اس بدن میں ترے دم سے ہے

تڑپنے پھڑکنے کی توفیق دے   دلِ مرتضیٰؓ، سوزِ صدیقؓ دے

جگر سے وہی تیر پھر پار کر   تمنا کو سینوں میں بیدار کر

ترے آسمانوں کے تاروں کی خیر   زمینوں کے شب زندہ داروں کی خیر

جوانوں کو سوزِ جگر بخش دے   مرا عشق، میری نظر بخش دے

مری ناؤ گرداب سے پار کر   یہ ثابت ہے تو اس کو سیّار کر

بتا مجھ کو اسرارِ مرگ و حیات   کہ تیری نگاہوں میں ہے کائنات

مرے دیدۂ تر کی بے خوابیاں   مرے دل کی پوشیدہ بے تابیاں

مرے نالۂ نیم شب کا نیاز   مری خلوت و انجمن کا گداز

اُمنگیں مری، آرزوئیں مری   اُمیدیں مری، جستجوئیں مری

مری فطرت آئینۂ روزگار   غزالانِ افکار کا مرغزار

مرا دل، مری رزم گاہِ حیات   گمانوں کے لشکر، یقیں کا ثبات

یہی کچھ ہے ساقی متاعِ فقیر   اسی سے فقیری میں ہوں میَں امیر

مرے قافلے میں لُٹا دے اسے

لُٹا دے، ٹھکانے لگا دے اسے!

Bread earned by any servitude,
For the watchman soul is poisoned food;
If you can eat and hold your head
High among men, you eat good bread.
Honour your Self, not fawn on the great,
Look down on Mahmud's pomp and state;
Kneel to God only: that prostration
Forbids as impious such oblation
To others. Earth's bright panoply,
This vale subject to death's decree,
This idol-house of eye and ear
Whose life is only belly-cheer,—
This is the Self's first halting-place,
Wayfarer, not your home! Its base
Cinder-heap was not your flame's source:
Not you by earth's, earth by your force
Exists. Pierce its huge rocks, and climb!
Burst the dark spells of space and time!
The Self, true lion of God, is given
For quarry the world, all earth, all heaven;
And new worlds wait, invisible
As yet: creation's heart beats still.
All things await your onset and
Your restless urge of brain and hand;
Time's revolutions have one goal,
To show you what is your own soul;
Oh lord of the world of foul and fair!
Your destiny how shall I declare?
Truth chokes, into words' tight garment thrust—
Truth the clear mirror, speech its rust;
The spirit's torch blazes in my breast,
The lamp of speech fails in the test—
My wings, if I mount one hair's breadth higher,
Must shrivel before that blinding fire!

خودی کے نگہباں کو ہے زہرِ ناب   وہ ناں جس سے جاتی رہے اس کی آب

وہی ناں ہے اس کے لیے ارجمند   رہے جس سے دنیا میں گردن بلند

درگزر محمود سے فروفالِ   خودی کو نگہ رکھ، ایازی نہ کر

وہی سجدہ ہے لائقِ اہتمام   کہ ہو جس سے ہر سجدہ تجھ پر حرام

یہ عالم، یہ ہنگامۂ رنگ و صوت   یہ عالم کہ ہے زیرِ فرمانِ موت

یہ عالم، یہ بت خانۂ چشم و گوش   جہاں زندگی ہے فقط خوردونوش

خودی کی یہ ہے منزلِ اولیں   مسافر! یہ تیرا نشیمن نہیں

تری آگ اس خاک داں سے نہیں   جہاں تجھ سے ہے، تو جہاں سے نہیں

بڑھے جا یہ کوہِ گراں توڑ کر   طلسم زمان و مکاں توڑ کر

خودی شیرِ مولا، جہاں اس کا صید   زمیں اس کی صید، آسماں اس کا صید

جہاں اور بھی ہیں ابھی بے نمود   کہ خالی نہیں ہے ضمیرِ وجود

ہر اک منتظر تیری یلغار کا   تری شوخئ فکر و کردار کا

یہ ہے مقصدِ گردشِ روزگار   کہ تیری خودی تجھ پہ ہو آشکار

تو ہے فاتحِ عالمِ خوب و زشت   تجھے کیا بتاؤں تری سرنوشت

حقیقت پہ ہے جامۂ حرف تنگ   حقیقت ہے آئینہ، گفتار زنگ

فروزاں ہے سینے میں شمعِ نفس   مگر تابِ گفتار کہتی ہے، بس!

اگر یک سرِ مُوئے برتر پَرَم

فروغِ تجلّی بسوزد پَرَم

45. Time

WHAT was, has faded: what is, is fading: but of these words
    few can tell the worth;
Time still is gaping with expectation of what is nearest its hour
    of birth.

New tidings slowly come drop by drop from my pitcher
    gurgling of time's new sights,
As I count over the beads strung out on my threaded rosary
    of days and nights.

With each man friendly, with each I vary, and have a new part
    at my command:
To one the rider, to one the courser, to one the whiplash of
    reprimand.

If in the circle you were not numbered, was it your own fault,
    or was it mine?
To humour no-one am I accustomed to keep untasted the
    midnight wine!

No planet-gazer can ever see through my winding mazes; for
    when the eye
That aims it sees by no light from Heaven, the arrow wavers
    and glances by.

زمانہ

جو تھا نہیں ہے، جو ہے نہ ہوگا، یہی ہے اک حرفِ محرمانہ

قریب تر ہے نمود جس کی، اُسی کا مشتاق ہے زمانہ

مری صراحی سے قطرہ قطرہ نئے حوادث ٹپک رہے ہیں

میں اپنی تسبیحِ روز و شب کا شمار کرتا ہوں دانہ دانہ

ہر ایک سے آشنا ہوں، لیکن جُدا جُدا رسم و راہ میری

کسی کا راکب، کسی کا مرکب، کسی کو عبرت کا تازیانہ

نہ تھا اگر تو شریکِ محفل، قصور میرا ہے یا کہ تیرا

مرا طریقہ نہیں کہ رکھ لوں کسی کی خاطر مئے شبانہ

مرے خم و پیچ کو نجومی کی آنکھ پہچانتی نہیں ہے

ہدف سے بیگانہ تیرا اُس کا، نظر نہیں جس کی عارفانہ

That is no dawn on the Western skyline—it is a bloodbath,
    that ruddy glow!
Await to-morrow; our yesterday and to-day are legends of
    long ago.

From Nature's forces their reckless science has stripped the
    garments away, until
At last its own nesting-place is scorched by the restless lightnings
    it cannot still:

To them the trade-wind belongs, the sky-way, to them the
    ocean, to them the ship—
It shall not serve them to calm the whirlpool by which their
    fate holds them in its grip!

But now a new world is being born, while this old one sinks
    out of sight of men,
This world the gamblers of Europe turned into nothing else
    than a gambling-den.

That man will still keep his lantern burning, however tempests
    blow strong and cold,
Whose soul is centred on high, whose temper the Lord has cast
    in the royal mould.

شفق نہیں مغربی اُفق پر، یہ جوئے خوں ہے! یہ جوئے خوں ہے!

طلوعِ فردا کا منتظر رہ کہ دوش و امروز ہے فسانہ

وہ فکرِ گستاخ جس نے عریاں کیا ہے فطرت کی طاقتوں کو

اُسی کی بیتاب بجلیوں سے خطر میں ہے اُس کا آشیانہ

ہوائیں اُن کی، فضائیں اُن کی، سمندر اُن کے، جہاز اُن کے

گرہ بھنور کی کھلے تو کیونکر؟ بھنور ہے تقدیر کا بہانہ!

جہانِ نو ہو رہا ہے پیدا، وہ عالم پیر مر رہا ہے

جسے فرنگی مقامروں نے بنا دیا ہے قمارخانہ

ہوا ہے گو تُند و تیز لیکن چراغ اپنا جلا رہا ہے

وہ مردِ درویش جس کو حق نے دیے ہیں اندازِ خسروانہ

46. *Gabriel and Satan*

GABRIEL

COMRADE of ancient days! how fares the world of sight and
    sound?

SATAN

In fire and rage and grief and pain and hope and longing
    drowned.

GABRIEL

No hour goes by in Paradise but your name is spoken there;
Is it not possible that rent robe be mended that you wear?

SATAN

Ah, Gabriel! you have never guessed my mystery; alas—
Maddened for ever I left upon Heaven's floor my broken glass.
Impossible, oh! impossible I should dwell here again;
Silent, how silent all this realm—no palace, no loud lane!
I whose despair is the fire by which the universe is stirred,
What should I do—all hope renounce, or hope yet in God's
    word?

GABRIEL

Your mutiny has put our high estate in Heaven to shame;
In the Creator's eye what credit now can angels claim?

جبریل و ابلیس

جبریل

ہمدمِ دیرینہ! کیسا ہے جہانِ رنگ و بو؟

ابلیس

سوز و ساز و درد و داغ و جستجوے و آرزو!

جبریل

ہر گھڑی افلاک پر رہتی ہے تیری گفتگو

کیا نہیں ممکن کہ تیرا چاکِ دامن ہو رفو؟

ابلیس

آہ اے جبریل! تو واقف نہیں اس راز سے

کر گیا سرمست مجھ کو ٹوٹ کر میرا سبو

اب یہاں میری گزر ممکن نہیں، ممکن نہیں

کس قدر خاموش ہے یہ عالم بے کاخ و کو!

جس کی نومیدی سے ہو سوزِ درونِ کائنات

اُس کے حق میں تَقْنَطُوْا اچھا ہے یا لَا تَقْنَطُوْا؟

جبریل

کھو دیئے انکار سے تو نے مقاماتِ بلند

چشمِ یزداں میں فرشتوں کی رہی کیا آبرو!

SATAN

But in Man's pinch of dust my daring spirit has breathed
    ambition,
The warp and woof of mind and reason are woven of my
    sedition.
The deeps of good and ill you only see from land's far verge:
Which of us is it, you or I, that dares the tempest's scourge?
Your ministers and your prophets are pale shades: the storms
    I teem
Roll down ocean by ocean, river by river, stream by stream!
Ask this of God, when next you stand alone within His sight—
Whose blood is it has painted Man's long history so bright?
In the heart of the Almighty like a pricking thorn I lie;
You only cry for ever God, oh God, oh God most high!

ابلیس

ہے مری جرأت سے مشتِ خاک میں ذوقِ نمو
میرے فتنے جامۂ عقل و خرد کا تاروپو!
دیکھتا ہے تو فقط ساحل سے رزمِ خیر و شر
کون طوفان کے طمانچے کھا رہا ہے، میں کہ تو؟
خضر بھی بے دست و پا، الیاس بھی بے دست و پا
میرے طوفاں یم بہ یم، دریا بہ دریا، جُو بہ جُو!
گر کبھی خلوت میسر ہو تو پوچھ اللہ سے
قصۂ آدم کو رنگیں کر گیا کس کا لہو؟
میں کھٹکتا ہوں دلِ یزداں میں کانٹے کی طرح
تو فقط اللہ ھُو، اللہ ھُو، اللہ ھُو!

47. *The Prayer-call*

ONE night among the planets
        The Star of Morning said—
'Has ever star seen slumber
        Desert Man's drowsy head?'

'Fate, being nimble-witted,'
        Bright Mercury returned,
'Served well that petty rebel—
        Tame sleep was what he earned!'

'Have we', asked Venus, 'nothing
        To talk about besides?
Or what is it to us, where
        That night-blind firefly hides?'
'A star', the Full Moon answered,
        'Is man, of terrene ray:
You walk the night in splendour,
        But so does he the day;

Let him once learn the joy of
        Outwatching night's brief span—
Higher than all the Pleiads
        The unfathomed dust of Man!
Closed in that dust a radiance
        Lies hidden, in whose clear light
Shall all the sky's fixed tenures
        And orbits fade from sight.'

—Suddenly rose the prayer-call,
        And overflowed heaven's lake;
That summons at which even
        Cold hearts of mountains quake.

اذان

اک رات ستاروں سے کہا نجمِ سحر نے
آدم کو بھی دیکھا ہے کسی نے کبھی بیدار؟
کہنے لگا مریخ، ادا فہم ہے تقدیر
ہے نیند ہی اس چھوٹے سے فتنے کو سزاوار
زہرہ نے کہا، اور کوئی بات نہیں کیا؟
اس کرمکِ شب کور سے کیا ہم کو سروکار!
بولا مہِ کامل کہ وہ کوکب ہے زمینی
تم شب کو نمودار ہو، وہ دن کو نمودار!
واقف ہو اگر لذتِ بیداریٔ شب سے
اُونچی ہے ثریّا سے بھی یہ خاکِ پُراسرار!
آغوش میں اس کی وہ تجلّی ہے کہ جس میں
کھو جائیں کے افلاک کے سب ثابت و سیّار!
ناگاہ فضا بانگِ اذاں سے ہوئی لب ریز
وہ نعرہ کہ ہِل جاتا ہے جس سے دلِ کہسار!

48. Sestet

THOUGH I have little of rhetorician's art,
Maybe these words will sink into your heart:

A quenchless crying on God through the boundless sky—
A dusty rosary, earth-bound litany—

So worship men self-knowing, drunk with God;
So worship priest, dead stone, and mindless clod.

قطعہ

انداز بیاں گرچہ بہت شوخ نہیں ہے

شاید کہ اُتر جائے ترے دل میں مری بات

یا وسعتِ افلاک میں تکبیرِ مسلسل

یا خاک کے آغوش میں تسبیح و مناجات!

وہ مذہبِ مردانِ خود آگاہ و خدا مست

یہ مذہبِ مُلّا و جمادات و نباتات

49. Love

THE martyrs of Love are not Muslim nor Paynim,
The manners of Love are not Arab nor Turk!
Some passion far other than Love was the power
That taught Ghazni's high ruler to dote on his slave.
When the spirit of Love has no place on the throne,
All wisdom and learning vain tricks and pretence!
Paying court to no king, by no king held in awe,
Love is freedom and honour, whose scorn of the world
Holds more than the magic that made Alexander
His fabulous mirror—its magic makes men.

محبت

شہیدِ محبت نہ کافر، نہ غازی   محبت کی رسمیں نہ ترکی، نہ تازی!

وہ کچھ اور شے ہے، محبت نہیں ہے   سکھاتی ہے جو غزنوی کو ایازی!

یہ جوہر اگر کارفرما نہیں ہے   تو ہیں علم و حکمت فقط شیشہ بازی!

نہ محتاجِ سلطاں، نہ مرعوبِ سلطاں   محبت ہے آزادی و بے نیازی!

مرا فقر بہتر ہے اسکندری سے

یہ آدم گری ہے، وہ آئینہ سازی!

50. At Napoleon's Tomb

STRANGE, strange the fates that govern
    This world of stress and strain,
But in the fires of action
    Fate's mysteries are made plain.

The sword of Alexander
    Rose sun-like from that blaze
To make the peaks of Alwand
    Run molten in its rays.

Action's loud storm called Timur's
    All-conquering torrent down—
And what to such wild billows
    Are fortune's smile or frown?

The prayers of God's folk treading
    The battlefield's red sod,
Forged in that flame of action
    Become the voice of God!

But only a brief moment
    Is granted to the brave—
One breath or two, whose wage is
    The long nights of the grave.

Then since at last the valley
    Of silence is our goal,
Beneath this vault of heaven
    Let our deeds' echoes roll!

نپولین کے مزار پر

راز ہے، راز ہے تقدیرِ جہانِ تگ و تاز

جوشِ کردار سے کھُل جاتے ہیں تقدیر کے راز

جوشِ کردار سے شمشیرِ سکندر کا طلوع

کوہِ الوند ہوا جس کی حرارت سے گداز

جوشِ کردار سے تیمور کا سیلِ ہمہ گیر

سیل کے سامنے کیا شے ہے نشیب اور فراز

صفِ جنگاہ میں مردانِ خدا کی تکبیر

جوشِ کردار سے بنتی ہے خدا کی آواز

ہے مگر فرصتِ کردار نفس یا دو نفس

عوضِ یک دو نفس قبر کی شب ہائے دراز!

'عاقبت، منزلِ ما وادئ خاموشان است

حالیا غلغلہ در گنبدِ افلاک انداز!'

51. To the Punjab Peasant

WHAT is this life of yours, tell me its mystery—
Trampled in dust is your ages-old history!
Deep in that dust has been smothered your flame—
Wake, and hear dawn its high summons proclaim!
Creatures of dust from the soil may draw bread:
Not in that darkness is Life's river fed!
Base will his metal be held, who on earth
Puts not to trial his innermost worth!
Break all the idols of tribe and of caste,
Break the old customs that fetter men fast!
Here is true victory, here is faith's crown—
One creed and one world, division thrown down!
Cast on the soil of your clay the heart's seed:
Promise of harvest to come is that seed!

پنجاب کے دہقان سے

بتا کیا تری زندگی کا ہے راز   ہزاروں برس سے ہے تو خاک باز!

اسی خاک میں دب گئی تیری آگ   سحر کی اذاں ہوگئی، اب تو جاگ!

زمیں میں ہے گو خاکیوں کی برات   نہیں اس اندھیرے میں آبِ حیات!

زمانے میں جھوٹا ہے اُس کا نگیں   جو اپنی خودی کو پرکھتا نہیں

بُتانِ شعوب و قبائل کو توڑ   رسومِ کہن کے سلاسل کو توڑ

یہی دینِ محکم، یہی فتحِ باب   کہ دنیا میں توحید ہو بے حجاب!

بخاکِ بدن دانۂ دل فشاں

کہ ایں دانہ دارد ز حاصل نشاں!

52. Nadir Shah of Afghanistan

LADEN with pearls departed from the presence-hall of God
That cloud that makes the pulse of life stir in the rose-bud's vein;
And on its way saw Paradise, and trembled with desire
That on such exquisite abode it might descend in rain.
A voice sounded from Paradise: 'They wait for you afar,
Kabul and Ghazni and Herat, and their new-springing grass;
Scatter the tear from Nadir's eye on the poppy's burning scar,
That never more may be put out the poppy's glowing fire!'

‏‏

نادرشاہ افغان

حضورِ حق سے چلالے کے لولوئے لالا

وہ ابر جس سے رگِ گل ہے مثلِ تارِ نفس

بہشت راہ میں دیکھا تو ہوگیا بیتاب

عجب مقام ہے، جی چاہتا ہے جاؤں برس

صدا بہشت سے آئی کہ منتظر ہے ترا

ہرات و کابل و غزنی کا سبزۂ نورس!

سرشکِ دیدۂ نادر بہ داغِ لالہ فشاں!

چناں کہ آتشِ اُو را دگر فرو نہ نشاں!

53. The Tartar's Dream

PRAYER-MAT and priestly turban have turned footpad,
With wanton boys' bold glances men are flattered;
The Church's mantle and the creed in shreds,
The robe of State and nation torn and tattered.
I cling to faith—but may its spark not soon
Lie quenched under these rubbish-heaps thick-scattered!
Bokhara's humble dust and Samarkand's
The turbulent billows of many winds have battered.

A gem set in a ring of misery
That circles me on every side, am I.

Suddenly quivered the dust of Samarkand,
And from an ancient tomb a light shone, pure
As the first gleam of daybreak, and a voice
Was heard:—'I am the spirit of Timur!
Chains may hold fast the men of Tartary,
But God's firm purposes no bonds endure;
Is this what life holds—that Turania's peoples
All hope in one another must abjure?

Call in the soul of man a new fire to birth!
Cry a new revolution over the earth!'

تاتاری کا خواب

کہیں سجادہ و عمامہ رہزن   کہیں ترسا بچوں کی چشم بے باک!

ردائے دین و ملّت پارہ پارہ   قبائے ملک و دولت چاک در چاک!

مرا ایماں تو ہے باقی، و لیکن   نہ کھا جائے کہیں شعلے کو خاشاک!

ہوائے تند کی موجوں میں محصور   سمرقند و بخارا کی کفِ خاک!

'بگردا گردِ خود چندانکہ بینم

بلا انگشتری و من نگینم'

یکایک ہل گئی خاکِ سمرقند   اُٹھا تیمور کی تربت سے اک نور

شفق آمیز تھی اُس کی سفیدی   صدا آئی کہ 'میں ہوں روحِ تیمور'

اگر محصور ہیں مردانِ تاتار   نہیں اللہ کی تقدیر محصور

تقاضا زندگی کا کیا یہی ہے   کہ تورانی ہو تورانی سے مہجور؟

'خودی راسوز و تابے دیگرے دہ

جہاں را انقلابے دیگرے دۂ

54. Cinema

CINEMA—or new fetish-fashioning,
Idol-making and mongering still?
Art, men called that olden voodoo—
Art, they call this mumbo-jumbo;
That—antiquity's poor religion:
This—modernity's pigeon-plucking;
That—earth's soil: this—soil of Hades;
Dust, their temple; ashes, ours.

سنیما

وہی بُت فروشی، وہی بُت گری ہے   سنیما ہے یا صنعتِ آزری ہے؟

وہ صنعت نہ تھی، شیوۂ کافری تھا   یہ صنعت نہیں، شیوۂ ساحری ہے

وہ مذہب تھا اقوامِ عہدِ کہن کا   یہ تہذیبِ حاضر کی سوداگری ہے

وہ   دنیا کی مٹی، یہ دوزخ کی مٹی

وہ بت خانہ خاکی، یہ خاکستری ہے!

55. *To the Punjab Pirs*

I STOOD by the Reformer's tomb: that dust
Whence here below an orient splendour breaks,
Dust before whose least speck stars hang their heads,
Dust shrouding that high knower of things unknown
Who to Jehangir would not bend his neck,
Whose ardent breath fans every free heart's ardour,
Whom Allah sent in season to keep watch
In India on the treasure-house of Islam.
I craved the saints' gift, other-worldliness;
For my eyes saw, yet dimly. Answer came:
'Closed is the long roll of the saints; this Land
Of the Five Rivers stinks in good men's nostrils.
God's people have no portion in that country
Where lordly tassel sprouts from monkish cap;
That cap bred passionate faith, this tassel breeds
Passion for playing pander to Government.'

پنجاب کے پیرزادوں سے

حاضر ہوا میں شیخ مجدّدؒ کی لحد پر

وہ خاک کہ ہے زیرِ فلک مطلعِ انوار

اس خاک کے ذروں سے ہیں شرمندہ ستارے

اس خاک میں پوشیدہ ہے وہ صاحبِ اسرار

گردن نہ جھکی جس کی جہانگیر کے آگے

جس کے نفسِ گرم سے ہے گرمئ احرار

وہ ہند میں سرمایۂ ملت کا نگہباں

اللہ نے بروقت کیا جس کو خبردار

کی عرض یہ میں نے عطا فقر ہو مجھ کو

آنکھیں مری بینا ہیں، ولیکن نہیں بیدار!

آئی یہ صدا سلسلۂ فقر ہوا بند

ہیں اہلِ نظر کشورِ پنجاب سے بیزار

عارف کا ٹھکانا نہیں وہ خطہ کہ جس میں

پیدا کلۂ فقر سے ہو طرّۂ دستار

باقی کلۂ فقر سے تھا ولولۂ حق

طرّوں نے چڑھایا نشۂ 'خدمتِ سرکار!'

56. Separation

THE sun is weaving with golden thread
A mantle of light about earth's head;
Creation hushed in ecstasy,
As in the presence of the Most High.
What can these know—stream, hill, moon, star—
Of separation's torturing scar?
Mine is this golden grief alone,
To this dust only is this grief known.

جدائی

دنیا کے لیے ردائے نوری   سورج بُنتا ہے تارِ زر سے

ہر شے کو نصیب ہے حضوری   عالم ہے خموش و مست گویا

کیا جانیں فراق و ناصبوری   دریا، کہسار، چاند، تارے

شایاں ہے مجھے غمِ جدائی

یہ خاک ہے محرمِ جدائی

57. *Satan's Petition*

To the Lord of the universe the Devil said:—
A firebrand Adam grows, that pinch of dust
Meagre-souled, plump of Flesh, in fine clothes trussed,
Brain ripe and subtle, heart not far from dead.
What the East's sacred law made men abjure,
The casuist of the West pronounces pure;
Knowest Thou not, the girls of Paradise see
And mourn their gardens turning wilderness?
For fiends its rulers serve the populace:
Beneath the heavens is no more need of me!

ابلیس کی عرضداشت

کہتا تھا عزازیل خداوندِ جہاں سے
پرکالۂ آتش ہوئی آدم کی کفِ خاک!

جاں لاغر و تن فربہ و ملبوس بدن زیب
دل نزع کی حالت میں، خرد پختہ و چالاک!

ناپاک جسے کہتی تھی مشرق کی شریعت
مغرب کے فقیہوں کا یہ فتویٰ ہے کہ ہے پاک!

تجھ کو نہیں معلوم کہ حورانِ بہشتی
ویرانیٔ جنت کے تصور سے ہیں غم ناک؟

جمہور کے ابلیس ہیں اربابِ سیاست
باقی نہیں اب میری ضرورت تہِ افلاک!

58. The Hawk

FAREWELL to this land of the earthbound, whose craving
It needs only water and food to appease!
Joy to my soul is the stillness of deserts—
My nature since time first began has scorned ease.
No languishing love-notes, no zephyr of springtime
For me, no fair flower-reaper: I must depart
From the nightingale's haunts, from these dwellers in gardens
Whose charms come too near to seducing my heart.
Those winds of the wilderness temper the sword
That soldiers of righteousness draw in the field;
It is not for quail nor for pigeon I hunger—
By hard vows the falcon's existence is steeled.
To swoop and retreat, and retreating to swoop—
Not seeking for prey, but to let the blood race!
I leave the tame region of eastward and west
To the partridge; blue sky for me, limitless space!
Through the kingdom of birds an Ascetic I roam:
The hawk builds no nest, for the hawk needs no home.

شاہیں

کیا میں نے اُس خاک داں سے کنارا   جہاں رزق کا نام ہے آب و دانہ

بیاباں کی خلوت خوش آتی ہے مجھ کو   ازل سے ہے فطرت مری راہبانہ

نہ بادِ بہاری، نہ گلچیں، نہ بلبل   نہ بیمارئ نغمۂ عاشقانہ

خیابانوں سے ہے پرہیز لازم   ادائیں ہیں ان کی بہت دلبرانہ

ہوائے بیاباں سے ہوتی ہے کاری   جواں مرد کی ضربت غازیانہ

حمام و کبوتر کا بھوکا نہیں میں   کہ ہے زندگی باز کی زاہدانہ

جھپٹنا، پلٹنا، پلٹ کر جھپٹنا   لہو گرم رکھنے کا ہے اک بہانہ

یہ پورب، یہ پچھم، چکوروں کی دنیا   مرا نیلگوں آسماں بیکرانہ

پرندوں کی دنیا کا درویش ہوں میں

کہ شاہیں بناتا نہیں آشیانہ!

59. Disciples in Revolt

Not a rushlight for us,—in our Master's
Fine windows electric lights blaze!
Town or village, the Muslim's a duffer—
To his *Brahmins* like idols he prays.
Not mere gifts—compound interest these saints want,
In each hair-shirt a usurer's dressed,
Who inherits his seat of authority
Like a crow in the eagle's old nest.

باغی مُرید

ہم کو تو میسر نہیں مٹی کا دیا بھی
گھر پیر کا بجلی کے چراغوں سے ہے روشن

شہری ہو، دہاتی ہو، مسلمان ہے سادہ
مانندِ بُتاں بِکتے ہیں کعبے کے برہمن

نذرانہ نہیں! سود ہے پیرانِ حرم کا
ہر خرقۂ سالوس کے اندر ہے مہاجن

میراث میں آئی ہے انھیں مسندِ ارشاد
زاغوں کے تصرّف میں عقابوں کے نشیمن!

PART III

ZARB-I-KALIM
THE ROD OF MOSES

60. Reason and Love

REASON once said to me:
   Moonstruck is Passion!
Passion once said to me:
   Reason would fashion
Mere worms in her book,
   Men bloodless and pale!
—Passion, a look;
   Reason, a veil.

Passion, hot breeze on
   The world-strife's fervescence—
The attribute Reason
   Shows, Passion the essence!
She is peace and long-during,
   Life, death, the reply
In her silence immuring
   To Reason's shrill cry.

She moulds on her wheel
   The king's oath, the priest's vows,
Her poor thrall with the seal
   And the sceptre endows;

She is dweller and dwelling,
   And country and hour,
And victory-compelling
   Faith is her dower.

By the path Love has branded
   Hearth-welcome is hidden,
The storm-wave commanded,
   The hugged shore forbidden;
No fruits in her season,
   But lightnings above—
The Book's offspring is Reason,
   Its parent is Love.

علم و عشق

علم نے مجھ سے کہا عشق ہے دیوانہ پن
عشق نے مجھ سے کہا علم ہے تخمین و ظن

بندۂ تخمین و ظن! کرمِ کتابی نہ بن
عشق سراپا حضور، علم سراپا حجاب!

عشق کی گرمی سے ہے معرکۂ کائنات
علم مقامِ صفات، عشق تماشائے ذات

عشق سکون و ثبات، عشق حیات و ممات
علم ہے پیدا سوال، عشق ہے پنہاں جواب!

عشق کے ہیں معجزات، سلطنت و فقر و دیں
عشق کے ادنیٰ غلام صاحبِ تاج و نگیں

عشق مکان و مکیں، عشق زمان و زمیں
عشق سراپا یقیں، اور یقیں فتحِ باب!

شرع محبت میں ہے عشرتِ منزل حرام
شورشِ طوفاں حلال، لذتِ ساحل حرام

عشق پہ بجلی حلال، عشق پہ حاصل حرام
علم ہے ابن الکتاب، عشق ہے اُمّ الکتاب!

61. Jehad

THIS is an age, our canonist's new dictum
Assures us, of the pen: in our world now
The sword has no more virtue.—Has it not reached
Our pious oracle's ear, that in the Mosque
Such sermonizing nowadays has grown
Rhymeless and reasonless? Where, in a Muslim's hand,
Will he find dagger or rifle? and if there were,
Our hearts have lost all memory of delight
In death. To one whose nerves falter at even
An infidel cut down, who would exclaim
'Die like a Muslim!' Preach relinquishment
Of such crusades to him whose bloody fist
Menaces earth! Europe, swathed cap-a-pie
In mail, mounts guard over her glittering reign
Of falsehood; we enquire of our divine,
So tender of Christendom: if for the East
War is unhallowed, is not war unhallowed
For Western arms? and if your goal be truth,
Is this the right road—Europe's faults all glossed,
And all Islam's held to so strict an audit?

جہاد

فتویٰ ہے شیخ کا یہ زمانہ قلم کا ہے
دنیا میں اب رہی نہیں تلوار کارگر
لیکن جناب شیخ کو معلوم کیا نہیں؟
مسجد میں اب یہ وعظ ہے بے سُود و بے اثر
تیغ و تفنگ دستِ مسلماں میں ہے کہاں
ہو بھی، تو دل ہیں موت کی لذّت سے بے خبر
کافر کی موت سے بھی لرزتا ہو جس کا دل
کہتا ہے کون اُسے کہ مسلماں کی موت مَر
تعلیم اُس کو چاہیے ترکِ جہاد کی
دنیا کو جس کے پنجۂ خونیں سے ہو خطر
باطل کے فال و فر کی حفاظت کے واسطے
یورپ زرہ میں ڈوب گیا دوش تا کمر
ہم پوچھتے ہیں شیخِ کلیسا نواز سے
مشرق میں جنگ شر ہے تو مغرب میں بھی ہے شر
حق سے اگر غرض ہے تو زیبا ہے کیا یہ بات
اسلام کا محاسبہ، یورپ سے درگزر؟

62. *Dazzled by Europe*

Your light is only Europe's light reflected:
You are four walls her architects have built,
A shell of dry mud with no tenant soul,
An empty scabbard chased with flowery gilt.

To your mind God's existence seems unproved:
Your own existence seems not proved to mine.
He whose Self shines like a gem, alone exists;
Take heed to it! I do not see yours shine.

افرنگ زدہ

ترا وجود سراپا تجلّیِ افرنگ
کہ تو وہاں کے عمارت گروں کی ہے تعمیر
مگر یہ پیکرِ خاکی خودی سے ہے خالی
فقط نیام ہے تُو، زرنگار و بے شمشیر!

تری نگاہ میں ثابت نہیں خدا کا وجود
مری نگاہ میں ثابت نہیں وجود ترا
وجود کیا ہے؟ فقط جوہرِ خودی کی نمود
کر اپنی فکر کہ جوہر ہے بے نمود ترا

63. *Islam in India*

ONLY identity of thought
    Keeps the Faith thriving—
Doctrine by whose means schism is brought
    Is impious striving;
And only the strong hand is fit
    To guard the creed:
Let no-one trust man's native wit
    To serve such need.
But that strength, preacher, we shall not
    Find *your* hand muster;
Go, and recite in some cool grot
    Your paternoster—

And there concoct some new Islam,
    Whose mystic kernel
Shall be a tame submissive calm,
    Despair eternal!
—In India, if bare leave be deigned
    His prayer-prostration,
Our dull priest thinks Islam has gained
    Emancipation.

ہندی اسلام

ہے زندہ فقط وحدتِ افکار سے ملّت
وحدت ہو فنا جس سے وہ الہام بھی الحاد
وحدت کی حفاظت نہیں بے قوتِ بازو
آتی نہیں کچھ کام یہاں عقلِ خداداد
اے مردِ خدا! تجھ کو وہ قوت نہیں حاصل
جا بیٹھ کسی غار میں اللہ کو کر یاد
مسکینی و محکومی و نومیدئ جاوید
جس کا یہ تصوف ہو وہ اسلام کر ایجاد
مُلّا کو جو ہے ہند میں سجدے کی اجازت
ناداں یہ سمجھتا ہے کہ اسلام ہے آزاد!

64. Fate

SATAN

Oh God, Creator! I did not hate your Adam,
That captive of Far-and-Near and Swift-and-Slow;
And what presumption could refuse to *You*
Obedience? If I would not kneel to him,
The cause was Your own fore-ordaining will.

GOD

When did that mystery dawn on you? before,
Or after your sedition?

SATAN

       After, oh brightness
Whence all the glory of all being flows.

GOD (to His angels)

See what a grovelling nature taught him this
Fine theorem! His not kneeling, he pretends,
Belonged to My fore-ordinance; gives his freedom
Necessity's base title;—wretch! his own
Consuming fire he calls a wreath of smoke.

تقدیر

(ابلیس و یزداں)

ابلیس

اے خدائے کن فکاں! مجھ کو نہ تھا آدم سے بَیر

آہ! وہ زندانیٔ نزدیک و دُور و دیر و زُود

حرفِ اِستکبار تیرے سامنے ممکن نہ تھا

ہاں، مگر تیری مشیّت میں نہ تھا میرا سجود

یزداں

کب کھُلا تجھ پر یہ راز؟ انکار سے پہلے کہ بعد؟

ابلیس

بعد! اے تیری تجلّی سے کمالاتِ وجود!

یزداں
(فرشتوں کی طرف دیکھ کر)

پستیٔ فطرت نے سکھلائی ہے یہ حجت اسے

کہتا ہے 'تیری مشیّت میں نہ تھا میرا سجود'

دے رہا ہے اپنی آزادی کو مجبوری کا نام

ظالم اپنے شعلۂ سوزاں کو خود کہتا ہے دود!

65. *The Way of Islam*

WHAT, shall I tell you then, is a Muslim's life?
Ecstasy's summit joined with profoundest thought!
Even its setting flames like a rising sun;
Single its hue, yet manifold age by age;
Neither with these times sharing their scorn of virtue,
Nor with times past their bondage to myth and magic,
Firm on eternal verity's bedrock standing—
Here is true life, no airy conceit of Plato!
Love, that the Spirit harbours, of loveliness
Mingles amid its elements with Iran's
Beauty of mind, Arabia's inward fire.

مدنیّتِ اسلام

بتاؤں تجھ کو مسلماں کی زندگی کیا ہے

یہ ہے نہایتِ اندیشہ و کمالِ جنوں

طلوع ہے صفتِ آفتاب اس کا غروب

یگانہ اور مثالِ زمانہ گوناگوں!

نہ اس میں عصرِ رواں کی حیا سے بیزاری

نہ اس میں عہدِ کہن کے فسانہ و افسوں

حقائقِ ابدی پر اساس ہے اس کی   یہ زندگی ہے، نہیں ہے طلسم افلاطوں!

عناصر اس کے ہیں روح القدس کا ذوقِ جمال   عجم کا حسنِ طبیعت، عرب کا سوزِ دروں!

66. Preaching of Islam in the West

THROUGH all the Western politeia
Religion withers to the roots;
For the white man, ties of blood and race
Are all he knows of brotherhood—
A Brahmin, in Britannia's sight,
Ascends no higher in life's scale

Because the creed of the Messiah
Has numbered him with its recruits;
All Britain one day might embrace
Muhammad's doctrine, if she would,
And yet the Muhammadan, luckless wight,
Be left as now beyond the pale.

اشاعتِ اسلام فرنگستان میں

ضمیر اس مدنیّت کا دیں سے ہے خالی

فرنگیوں میں اخوت کا ہے نسب پہ قیام

بلند تر نہیں انگریز کی نگاہوں میں

قبولِ دینِ مسیحی سے برہمن کا مقام

اگر قبول کرے، دینِ مصطفیٰؐ، انگریز

سیاہ روز مسلماں رہے گا پھر بھی غلام

67. Modern Man

Love fled, Mind stung him like a snake; he could not
    Force it to vision's will.
He tracked the orbits of the stars, yet could not
    Travel his own thoughts' world;
Entangled in the labyrinth of his science
    Lost count of good and ill;
Took captive the sun's rays, and yet no sunrise
    On life's thick night unfurled.

زمانۂ حاضر کا انسان

عشق ناپید و خرد ہے گردشِ صورتِ مآز

عقل کو تابِع فرمانِ نظر کر نہ سکا

ڈھونڈنے والا ستاروں کی گزرگاہوں کا

اپنے افکار کی دنیا میں سفر کر نہ سکا

اپنی حکمت کے خم و پیچ میں اُلجھا ایسا

آج تک فیصلۂ نفع و ضرر کر نہ سکا

جس نے سورج کی شعاعوں کو گرفتار کیا

زندگی کی شبِ تاریک سحر کر نہ سکا!

68. Eastern Nations

REALITY grows blurred to eyes whose vision
Servility and parrot-ways abridge.
Can Persia or Arabia suck new life
From Europe's culture, itself at the grave's edge?

69. A Student

GOD bring you acquainted with some storm!
No billows in your sea break in foam,
And never from books can you be weaned
Which you declaim, not comprehend.

اقوامِ مشرق

نظر آتے نہیں بے پردہ حقائق اُن کو
آنکھ جن کی ہوئی محکومی و تقلید سے کور
زندہ کرسکتی ہے ایران و عرب کو کیونکر
یہ فرنگی مدنیّت کو جو ہے خود لبِ گور!

طالبِ علم

خدا تجھے کسی طوفاں سے آشنا کردے
کہ تیرے بحر کی موجوں میں اضطراب نہیں
تجھے کتاب سے ممکن نہیں فراغ کہ تو
کتاب خواں ہے، مگر صاحبِ کتاب نہیں!

70. The Schools

THIS age that's with us is your angel of death,
Its bread and butter cares catch your soul's breath.
Your heart recoils from shock of combat; life
Is death, that deadens in men the joy of strife.
Learning estranged you from such exaltation
As would not let man's mind desert its station;
A falcon's eyes were yours by Nature's right,
Slavishness left them only a poor wren's sight,
And the schools hid from them those mysteries
That yield to hill's and desert's still assize.

71. A Question

ASK the wise men of Europe, who have hung
Their ring in the nose of Greece and Hindostan:
Is this their civilization's highest rung—
A childless woman and a jobless man?

مدرسہ

عصرِ حاضر ملک الموت ہے تیرا، جس نے
قبض کی روح تری دے کے تجھے فکرِ معاش
دل لرزتا ہے حریفانہ کشاکش سے ترا
زندگی موت ہے، کھو دیتی ہے جب ذوقِ خراش
اُس جنوں سے تجھے تعلیم نے بیگانہ کیا
جو یہ کہتا تھا خرد سے کہ بہانے نہ تراش
فیضِ فطرت نے تجھے دیدۂ شاہیں بخشا
جس میں رکھ دی ہے غلامی نے نگاہِ خفّاش
مدرسے نے تری آنکھوں سے چھپایا جن کو
خلوتِ کوہ و بیاباں میں وہ اسرار ہیں فاش!

ایک سوال

کوئی پوچھے حکیم یورپ سے
ہند و یوناں ہیں جس کے حلقہ بگوش
کیا یہی ہے معاشرت کا کمال؟
مرد بے کار و زن تہی آغوش!

72. *To my Poem*

I must complain of your self-flaunting airs—
My secrets, when you go unveiled, lie bare.
Instead of floating like a truant spark,
Seek out the fastness of some glowing heart!

73. *Paris Mosque*

WHAT should my eyes, but an architect's
Nimbleness, see in this shrine
Of the West? It knows nothing of God.
Mosque?—the Frankish illusionists
Have smuggled into the carcass
Of a shrine, an idol-hall's soul!

And who built this palace of idols?
The same robbers whose hands have turned
Damascus into a desert.

اپنے شعر سے

ہے گلہ مجھ کو تری لذّتِ پیدائی کا
تو ہوا فاش تو ہیں اب مرے اَسرار بھی فاش
شعلے سے ٹوٹ کے مثلِ شرر آوارہ نہ رہ
کر کسی سینۂ پُرسوز میں خلوت کی تلاش!

پیرس کی مسجد

مری نگاہ کمالِ ہنر کو کیا دیکھے
کہ حق سے یہ حرم مغربی ہے بیگانہ
حرم نہیں ہے، فرنگی کرشمہ بازوں نے
تنِ حرم میں چھپادی ہے روحِ بت خانہ
یہ بت کدہ انھیں غارت گروں کی ہے تعمیر
دمشق ہاتھ سے جن کے ہُوا ہے ویرانہ

74. To the Artists

Sun, moon and Jupiter shine their hour;
Your Self burns on, fed by Love's power.
Your creed knows nothing of race or hue:
No credit in white or black, or blue!
Where Selfhood droops, doubts fight ding-dong;
Where it blooms—a world of verse and song!
If your soul rot under slavery's blight,
Your art an idolater's soulless rite;
If sense of your own greatness sway you,
Legions of men and Jinn obey you!

اہلِ ہنر سے

مہرومہ و مشتری، چند نفس کا فروغ

عشق سے ہے پائدار تیری خودی کا وجود

تیرے حرم کا ضمیر اسود و احمر سے پاک

نگ ہے تیرے لیے سرخ و سپید و کبود

تیری خودی کا غیاب معرکۂ ذکر و فکر

تیری خودی کا حضور عالم شعر و سرود

روح اگر ہے تری رنجِ غلامی سے زار

تیرے ہنر کا جہاں دیر و طواف و سجود

اور اگر باخبر اپنی شرافت سے ہو

تیری سپہ انس و جن! تو ہے امیرِ جنود!

75. *Dawn in the Garden*

FLOWER

PERHAPS you fancied
My land far off, sky-herald!
   No, it is not far.

DEW

But only labouring wings
Prove earth not far from heaven!

DAWN

Softly as morning,
Not trampling its dewdrop pearls,
   Enter this garden.
Clasp hill and desert, yet still
Catch in your hands the sky's robe.

صبحِ چمن

پھول

شاید تو سمجھتی تھی وطن دور ہے میرا

اے قاصِد افلاک! نہیں! دور نہیں ہے!

شبنم

ہوتا ہے مگر محنتِ پرواز سے روشن

یہ نکتہ کہ گردوں سے زمیں دور نہیں ہے

صبح

مانندِ سحر صحنِ گلستاں میں قدم رکھ

آئے ترے پا گوہرِ شبنم تو نہ ٹوٹے

ہو کوہ و بیاباں سے ہم آغوش و لیکن

ہاتھوں سے ترے دامنِ افلاک نہ چھوٹے!

76. Persian Poetry

THE Persian Muse is mirthsome and heart-easing,
No whetstone for the sword-edge of the Self.
Better the song-bird of the dawn be still,
Than by her notes lull Flowerland into languor.
What use the patient axe that hews through mountains
Yet leaves Parvez and his proud throne unscathed?
This is an age, Iqbal, for carving flint:
From all glass-wares they show you, turn away.

شعرِ عجم

ہے شعرِ عجم گرچہ طرب ناک و دل آویز

اس شعر سے ہوتی نہیں شمشیرِ خودی تیز

افسردہ اگر اس کی نوا سے ہو گلستاں

بہتر ہے کہ خاموش رہے مرغِ سحر خیز

وہ ضرب اگر کوہ شکن بھی ہو تو کیا ہے

جس سے متزلزل نہ ہوئی دولتِ پرویز

اقبال یہ ہے خارہ تراشی کا زمانہ

'از ہر چہ بآئینہ نمایند بہ پرہیز!'

77. *India's Artists*

THEIR fantasy, death-bed of love and passion;
Their sunless minds the burial-vaults of nations;
In their idolatrous halls Death's portrait hangs,
Their art, like a priest's soul, sickens of life;

They hide from mortal eyes the heavens' high places,
Their gift is drowsy spirit and itching flesh.
Oh, India's painters, poets, and story-tellers!
The female sits astride their quivering nerves.

78. *Dancing*

To Europe leave the dance of serpent limb:
The prophet's power is born of the spirit's dance.
That breeds the craving flesh, the sweating palm,
This breeds the race of pilgrim and of prince.

ہنروارانِ ہند

عشق و مستی کا جنازہ ہے تخیّل ان کا
ان کے اندیشۂ تاریک میں قوموں کے مزار
موت کی نقش گری ان کے صنم خانوں میں
زندگی سے ہنر ان برہنوں کا بیزار
چشمِ آدم سے چھپاتے ہیں مقاماتِ بلند
کرتے ہیں روح کو خوابیدہ، بدن کو بیدار
ہند کے شاعر و صورت گر و افسانہ نویس
آہ! بیچاروں کے اعصاب پہ عورت ہے سوار!

رقص

چھوڑ یورپ کے لیے رقصِ بدن کے خم و پیچ
روح کے رقص میں ہے ضربِ کلیم اللّٰہی!
صلہ اُس رقص کا ہے تشنگیٔ کام و دہن
صلہ اِس رقص کا درویشی و شاہنشاہی!

79. *The Voice of Karl Marx*

Your chessmatch of research and erudition—
Your comedy of debate and disputation!—
The world has no more patience left to watch
This comedy of threadbare speculation.
What after all, sapient economists,
Is to be found in your biblification?

A comedy of nicely-flowing curves,
A sort of Barmecidal invitation.
In the idolatrous shrines of the Occident,
Its pulpits and its seats of education,
Greed and its murderous crimes are masked under
Your knavish comedy of cerebration.

80. *Revolution*

Death to man's soul is Europe, death is Asia
To man's will: neither feels the vital current.
In men's hearts stirs a revolution's torrent;
Maybe our old world too is nearing death.

کارل مارکس کی آواز

یہ علم و حکمت کی مہرہ بازی، یہ بحث و تکرار کی نمائش

نہیں ہے اب گوارا دنیا کو پرانے افکار کی نمائش

تری کتابوں میں اے حکیمِ معاش رکھا ہی کیا ہے آخر

خطوطِ خم دارؔ کی نمائش، مریز و کج دار کی نمائش

جہانِ مغرب کے بت کدوں میں،کلیساؤں میں، مدرسوں میں

ہوس کی خوں ریزیاں چھپاتی ہے عقلِ عیّار کی نمائش

انقلاب

نہ ایشیا میں نہ یورپ میں سوزوسازِ حیات

خودی کی موت ہے یہ، اور وہ ضمیر کی موت

دلوں میں ولولۂ انقلاب ہے پیدا

قریب آ گئی شاید جہانِ پیر کی موت!

81. Flattery

THOUGH versed in this world's business *I* am not,
There are shrewd folk who always know what's what.
Swim with the tide, flatter Their Excellencies
Of the new dispensation that commences!
(Would it be more veracious, or-polite,
I wonder, to call an owl 'the falcon of night'?)

82. Government Jobs

ONE hermit's eyes grew wet with watching how you fell,
        Poor Muslim, under England's spell.
God give you joy of those high offices, to taste
        Whose sweets you laid your own soul waste!
But here's a thing you cannot, try as you will, disguise
        From any knowing pair of eyes:
No slave is given a partnership in England's reign—
        She only wants to buy his brain.

خوشامد

میں کارِ جہاں سے نہیں آگاہ، و لیکن
ارباب نظر سے نہیں پوشیدہ کوئی راز
کر تُو بھی حکومت کے وزیروں کی خوشامد
دستور نیا، اور نئے دَور کا آغاز
معلوم نہیں ہے یہ خوشامد کہ حقیقت
کہہ دے کوئی اُلو کو اگر 'رات کا شہباز!'

مناصب

ہوا ہے بندۂ مومن فسونئ افرنگ
اسی سبب سے قلندر کی آنکھ ہے نم ناک
ترے بلند مناصب کی خیر ہو، یارب!
کہ ان کے واسطے تو نے کیا خودی کو ہلاک

مگر یہ بات چھپائے سے چھُپ نہیں سکتی
سمجھ گئی ہے اسے ہر طبیعتِ چالاک
'شریکِ حکم غلاموں کو کر نہیں سکتے
خریدتے ہیں فقط اُن کا جوہرِ ادراک!'

83. Europe and the Jews

UNBRIDLED luxury, State pomp and pride,
    Rich commerce; but to dwell inside
That lampless breasts all tranquil thoughts refuse.
Dark is the white man's country with the grime
    Of engines, no valley that might see
Splendour descending on a burning tree;
A civilization sick before its prime,
    At its last gasp—leaving maybe
For caretakers of Christendom, the Jews.

84. Slave Mentality

POETS come forth, scholars too, and philosophers
—Lands are not empty in seasons of slavery—,
Each with his own special crotchets to air,
But all piously joining in one common knavery:

They educate lions to tremble like deer,
Till less than a leonine legend of bravery
Lingers,—they reconcile serfs to their serfdom
Under colour of learnedly clearing our minds.

یورپ اور یہود

یہ عیشِ فراواں، یہ حکومت، یہ تجارت
دل سینۂ بے نور میں محرومِ تسلّی

تاریک ہے افرنگ مشینوں کے دھوئیں سے
یہ وادئ ایمن نہیں شایانِ تجلّی

ہے نزع کی حالت میں یہ تہذیبِ جواں مرگ
شاید ہوں کلیسا کے یہودی متوَلّی!

نفسیاتِ غلامی

شاعر بھی ہیں پیدا، غلامی بھی، حکما بھی
خالی نہیں قوموں کی غلامی کا زمانہ

مقصد ہے ان اللہ کے بندوں کا مگر ایک
ہر ایک ہے گو شرحِ معانی میں یگانہ

''بہتر ہے کہ شیروں کو سکھادیں رمِ آہو
باقی نہ رہے شیر کی شیری کا فسانۂ

کرتے ہیں غلاموں کو غلامی پہ رضامند
تاویلِ مسائل کو بناتے ہیں بہانہ

85. *Bolshevik Russia*

UNSEARCHABLY God's edicts move; who knows
What thoughts are stirring deep in the world-mind
Those are appointed to pull down, who lately
Held it salvation to protect, the priests;
On godless Russia the command descends:
Smite all the Baals and Dagons of the Church!

86. *To-day and To-morrow*

No claims to the future, its joy or its sorrow,
Has he in whose soul no hot passion burns now;
Unworthy the tumult and strife of to-morrow
That nation to whose will to-day does not bow.

87. *The East*

THE poppy heard my song and tore her mantle;
The morning breeze is still in search of a garden.
Ill lodged in Ataturk or Reza Shah,
The soul of the East is still in search of a body.
This thing I am may merit chastisement;
Only—the world is still in search of a gibbet.

بلشویک روس

روش قضائے الٰہی کی ہے عجیب و غریب
خبر نہیں کہ ضمیرِ جہاں میں ہے کیا بات
ہوئے ہیں کسر چلیپا کے واسطے مامور
وہی کہ حفظِ چلیپا کو جانتے تھے نجات
یہ وہی دہریتِ روس پر ہوئی نازل
کہ توڑ ڈال کلیسائیوں کے لات و منات!

آج اور کل

وہ کل کے غم و عیش پہ کچھ حق نہیں رکھتا
جو آج خود افروز و جگر سوز نہیں ہے
وہ قوم نہیں لائقِ ہنگامۂ فردا
جس قوم کی تقدیر میں امروز نہیں ہے!

مشرق

مری نوا سے گریبانِ لالہ چاک ہوا
نسیمِ صبح چمن کی تلاش میں ہے ابھی
نہ مصطفٰی نہ رضا شاہ میں نمود اس کی
کہ روحِ شرق بدن کی تلاش میں ہے ابھی
مری خودی بھی سزا کی ہے مستحق لیکن
زمانہ دار و رسن کی تلاش میں ہے ابھی

88. *European Politics*

THY rival, God! the Frankish statecraft is,
Though none but rich and great join in its worship.
One sole Archfiend didst Thou from flame make: it
Has formed from dust two hundred thousand fiends.

89. *To the Egyptians*

NONE other than the Sphinx, the Dread One, lord
Of the secrets of old time, taught me this: Strength
That in one hour can swerve the fates of nations
Admits no puzzling intellect for rival,
Though many in each age are its manifestations—
Now Moses' rod, and now Muhammad's sword.

سیاستِ افرنگ

تری حریف ہے یارب سیاستِ افرنگ
مگر ہیں اس کے پجاری فقط امیر و رئیس
بنایا ایک ہی ابلیس آگ سے تو نے
بنائے خاک سے اُس نے دو صد ہزار ابلیس!

اہلِ مصر سے

خود ابوالہول نے یہ نکتہ سکھایا مجھ کو
وہ ابوالہول کہ ہے صاحبِ اسرارِ قدیم
دفعتہً جس سے بدل جاتی ہے تقدیرِ اُمم
ہے وہ قوّت کہ حریف اس کی نہیں عقلِ حکیم
ہر زمانے میں دگرگوں ہے طبیعت اس کی
کبھی شمشیرِ محمؐد ہے، کبھی چوبِ کلیمؑ!

90. Abyssinia
(18th August 1935)

THOSE vultures of the West have yet to learn
What poisons lurk in Abyssinia's corpse,
That rotting carcass ready to fall in pieces.

Civilization's zenith, nadir of virtue;
In our world pillage is the nations' trade,
Each wolf aprowl for inoffensive lambs.

Woe to the shining honour of the Church,
For Rome has shivered it in the market-place!
Sharp-clawed, oh Holy Father, is the truth.

ابی سینیا

(۱۸؍اگست ۱۹۳۵ء)

یورپ کے کرگسوں کو نہیں ہے ابھی خبر

ہے کتنی زہرناک ابی سینیا کی لاش

ہونے کو ہے یہ مردۂ دیرینہ قاش قاش!

تہذیب کا کمال شرافت کا ہے زوال

غارت گری جہاں میں ہے اقوام کی معاش

ہرگرگ کو ہے برۂ معصوم کی تلاش!

اے وائے آبروئے کلیسا کا آئینہ

روما نے کردیا سرِ بازار پاش پاش

پیرِ کلیسا! یہ حقیقت ہے دلخراش!

91. *Satan to his Political Offspring*

ENMESH in politics the Brahmin—from
Their ancient altars the twice-born expel!
The man who famine-racked still fears no
death—
Muhammad's spirit from his breast expel!
With Frankish daydreams fill Arabia's brain—
Islam from Yemen and Hejaz expel!
The Afghan reveres religion: take this cure—
His teachers from their mountain-glens expel!
Tear from the true-believers their traditions—
From Khutan's meadows the musk-deer expel!
Iqbal's breath fans the poppy into flame—
Such mistrels from the flower-garden expel!

ابلیس کا فرمان اپنے سیاسی فرزندوں کے نام

لاکر برہمنوں کو سیاست کے پیچ میں

زناریوں کو دَیرِ کہن سے نکال دو

وہ فاقہ کش کہ موت سے ڈرتا نہیں ذرا

روحِ محمؐد اس کے بدن سے نکال دو

فکرِ عرب کو دے کے فرنگی تخیّلات

اسلام کو حجاز و یمن سے نکال دو

افغانیوں کی غیرتِ دیں کا ہے یہ علاج

مُلّا کو اُن کے کوہ و دمن سے نکال دو

اہلِ حرم سے اُن کی روایات چھین لو

آہو کو مرغزارِ خُتن سے نکال دو

اقبالؔ کے نفس سے ہے لالے کی آگ تیز

ایسے غزل سرا کو چمن سے نکال دو!

92. *An Eastern League of Nations*

CONQUERED the waters,
    Conquered the air—
Why should old heaven
    Changed looks not wear?
Europe's imperialists
    Dreamed—but their dream
Soothsayers soon may
    Read a new way!
Asia's Geneva
    Let Teheran be—
Earth's book of fate new
    Statutes may see.

93. *Everlasting Monarchy*

A DIVER after pearls Nature made me,
Though wary of the abysses of the State.
Whomever its legerdemain may captivate,
She sets a term to every monarchy;
Farhad's hill-hewing labour still lives on,
Parvez' conquering might is dead and gone.

94. *Europe and Syria*

THIS land of Syria gave the West a Prophet
Of purity and pity and innocence;
And Syria from the West as recompense
Gets dice and drink and troops of prostitutes.

جمیعتِ اقوامِ مشرق

پانی بھی مُسخّر ہے، ہوا بھی ہے مُسخّر

کیا ہو جو نگاہِ فلک پیر بدل جائے

دیکھا ہے ملوکیتِ افرنگ نے جو خواب

ممکن ہے کہ اُس خواب کی تعبیر بدل جائے

طہران ہو اگر عالمِ مشرق کا جنیوا

شاید کرۂ ارض کی تقدیر بدل جائے!

سلطانئ جاوید

غوّاص تو فطرت نے بنایا ہے مجھے بھی

لیکن مجھے اعماقِ سیاست سے ہے پرہیز

فطرت کو گوارا نہیں سلطانئ جاوید

ہر چند کہ یہ شعبدہ بازی ہے دل آویز

فرہاد کی خاراشکنی زندہ ہے اب تک

باقی نہیں دنیا میں ملوکیتِ پرویز!

یورپ اور سوریا

فرنگیوں کو عطا خاکِ سوریا نے کیا

نبیّ عفت و غم خواری و کم آزاری

صلہ فرنگ سے آیا ہے سوریا کے لیے

مَے و قمار و ہجومِ زنانِ بازاری!

95. Mussolini

(To his rivals east and west.)

WHAT, are crimes like Mussolini's so unheard of in this age?
Why should they put Europe's goodies into such a silly rage?
Need the pot feel so indignant when the kettle wears a blot?
We are Culture's twin utensils—I the kettle, you the pot.
You have watched my lust for conquest and dominion with a
    frown—
But have you not knocked the brittle walls of feeble countries
    down?

To whose empires is that clever piece of trickery so dear,
By which royal seats survive but kings and kingdoms disappear

We, the children of the Caesars, strove to water heath and
    sand—
You could never bear to leave untaxed the earth's most barren
    land;
You have plundered tents of nomads of the little wealth they
    own,
You have plundered peasant ploughlands, you have plundered
    crown and throne,
And that looting and that killing—in a civilizing way—
Yesterday you, you defended! I defend it now to-day.

مسولینی

(اپنے مشرقی اور مغربی حریفوں سے)

کیا زمانے سے نرالا ہے مسولینی کا جُرم؟

بے محل بگڑا ہے معصومانِ یورپ کا مزاج

میں پھٹکتا ہوں تو چھلنی کو بُرا لگتا ہے کیوں

ہیں سبھی تہذیب کے اوزار! تو چھلنی، میں چھاج

میرے سودائے مُلوکیت کو ٹھکراتے ہو تم

تم نے کیا توڑے نہیں کمزور قوموں کے زُجاج؟

یہ عجائب شعبدے کس کی مُلوکیت کے ہیں

راجدھانی ہے، مگر باقی نہ راجا ہے نہ راج

آل سیزر چوب نَے کی آبیاری میں رہے

اور تم دنیا کے نجبر بھی نہ چھوڑو بے خراج!

تم نے لوٹے بے نوا صحرانشینوں کے خیام

تم نے لوٹی کشتِ دہقاں، تم نے لوٹے تخت و تاج!

پردۂ تہذیب میں غارت گری، آدم کُشی

کل روارکھی تھی تم نے، میں روارکھتا ہوں آج!

96. Reproach

YOUR fate, poor helpless India, there's no telling—
Always the brightest jewel in someone's crown;
Your peasant a carcass spewed up from the grave,
Whose coffin is mouldering still beneath the sod.
Mortgaged to the alien, soul and body too,
Alas—the dweller vanished with the dwelling—,

Enslaved to Britain you have kissed the rod:
It is not Britain I reproach, but you.

97. Civilization's Clutches

IQBAL has no doubt of Europe's humaneness: she
Sheds tears for all peoples groaning beneath oppression;
Her reverend churchmen furnish her liberally
With wiring and bulbs for moral illumination.
And yet, my heart burns for Syria and Palestine,
And finds for this knotty puzzle no explanation—
Enlarged from the 'savage grasp' of the Turks, they pine,
Poor things, in the clutches now of 'civilization'.

گِلہ

معلوم کسے ہند کی تقدیر کہ اب تک
بیچارہ کسی تاج کا تابندہ نگیں ہے
دہقاں ہے کسی قبر کا اُگلا ہوا مُردہ
بوسیدہ کفن جس کا ابھی زیرِ زمیں ہے
جاں بھی گروِ غیر، بدن بھی گروِ غیر
افسوس کہ باقی نہ مکاں ہے نہ مکیں ہے
یورپ کی غلامی پہ رضامند ہوا تُو
مجھ کو تو گِلہ تجھ سے ہے، یورپ سے نہیں ہے!

دامِ تہذیب

اقبالؔ کو شک اس کی شرافت میں نہیں ہے
ہر ملّتِ مظلوم کا یورپ ہے خریدار
یہ پیر کلیسا کی کرامت ہے کہ اس نے
بجلی کے چراغوں سے منور کیے افکار
جلتا ہے مگر شام و فلسطیں پہ مرا دل
تدبیر سے کھلتا نہیں یہ عقدۂ دشوار
تُرکانِ 'جفاپیشہ' کے پنجے سے نکل کر
بیچارے ہیں تہذیب کے پھندے میں گرفتار!

98. League of Nations

SHE'S been at her last gasp, poor wretch, for days
(May telling ill news not bring ill news to me!)—
Yet though her fate seems sealed, the Church still prays
Her fate may be averted. Well, maybe
After all the Old Man of Europe's drab will rally
A few days longer, with the devil for ally!

99. Syria and Palestine

HEAVEN'S blessing on those brazen Frenchmen shine!
Aleppo's rare glass brims with their red wine.
—If the Jew claims the soil of Palestine,
Why not the Arab Spain? Some new design
Must have inflamed our English potentates;
This is no story of oranges, honey, or dates.

100. Political Leaders

ON political leaders what hopes can we fix?
They are wedded to dust, in the dust play their tricks,
Their gaze always fastened on maggots and flies,
A web like the spider's their ladder to rise.
That caravan's happy whose chief is endowed
With thoughts high as angels', and temper as proud.

جمعیتِ اقوام

بیچاری کئی روز سے دم توڑ رہی ہے
ڈر ہے خبرِ بد نہ مرے منہ سے نکل جائے
تقدیر تو مُبرم نظر آتی ہے و لیکن
پیرانِ کلیسا کی دعا یہ ہے کہ ٹل جائے
ممکن ہے یہ داشتہ پیرکِ افرنگ
ابلیس کے تعویذ سے کچھ روز سنبھل جائے!

شام و فلسطین

رندانِ فرانسیس کا میخانہ سلامت
پُر ہے مئے گلرنگ سے ہر شیشہ حلب کا
ہے خاکِ فلسطیں پہ یہودی کا اگر حق
ہسپانیہ پر حق نہیں کیوں اہلِ عرب کا؟
مقصد ہے ملوکیتِ انگلیس کا کچھ اور
قصہ نہیں نارنج کا یا شہد و رُطب کا!

سیاسی پیشوا

اُمید کیا ہے سیاست کے پیشواؤں سے
یہ خاک باز ہیں، رکھتے ہیں خاک سے پیوند
ہمیشہ مور و مگس پر نگاہ ہے ان کی
جہاں میں ہے صفتِ عنکبوت ان کی کمند
خوشاوہ قافلہ، جس کے امیر کی ہے متاع
تخیّلِ ملکوتی و جذبہ ہائے بلند!

101. Slaves' Prayers

'WHY do your priests', said to me after prayers
A Turkish hero of the faith, 'drag out.

Their genuflexions so?'—He little knew,
That free-born Muslim, that plain warrior,
What kind of thing slaves' prayers are! In this world
A thousand tasks lie ready for the free,
In whom the love of high deeds burns and forges
The nations and their laws; but that fire never
Touches the bondman's limbs, whose nights and days
Stand still under an interdict. If our
Prostrations are long-drawn, why should you wonder?
What have the poor to do but kneel and pray?
—God teach His ministers in India
A way of worship that shall be to all
His people an evangel of new life!

غلاموں کی نماز

(ترکی وفدِ ہلالِ احمر لاہور میں)

کہا مجاہدِ ترکی نے مجھ سے بعدِ نماز
طویل سجدہ ہیں کیوں اس قدر تمھارے امام؟
وہ سادہ مردِ مجاہد، وہ مومنِ آزاد
خبر نہ تھی اُسے کیا چیز ہے نمازِ غلام
ہزار کام ہیں مردانِ حُر کو دنیا میں
انھیں کے ذوقِ عمل سے ہیں اُمتوں کے نظام
بدن غلام کا سوزِ عمل سے ہے محروم
کہ ہے مرؤر غلاموں کے روزوشب پہ حرام
طویل سجدہ اگر ہیں تو کیا تعجب ہے
ورائے سجدہ غریبوں کو اور کیا ہے کام
خدا نصیب کرے ہند کے اماموں کو
وہ سجدہ جس میں ہے ملّت کی زندگی کا پیام!

102. East and West

SLAVERY, slavishness, the root of our
Disease; of theirs, that Demos holds all power;
Heart-malady or brain-malady has oppressed
Man's whole world, sparing neither East nor West.

103. Psychology of Power
(The 'Reforms')

THIS pity is the pitiless fowler's mask;
All the fresh notes I sang—of no avail!
Now he drops withered flowers in our cage, as though
To reconcile his jailbirds to their jail.

مشرق و مغرب

یہاں مرض کا سبب ہے غلامی و تقلید
وہاں مرض کا سبب ہے نظامِ جمہوری
نہ مشرق اس سے بَری ہے، نہ مغرب اس سے بَری
جہاں میں عام ہے قلب و نظر کی رنجوری!

نفسیاتِ حاکمی

(اصلاحات)

یہ مہر ہے بے مہری صیّاد کا پردہ
آئی نہ مرے کام مری تازہ صفیری
رکھنے لگا مرجھائے ہوئے پھول قفس میں
شاید کہ اسیروں کو گوارا ہو اسیری!

PART IV

ARMAGHAN-I-HEJAZ

THE GIFT OF HEJAZ

104. Satan's Parliament

SATAN

THE elements weave their ancient dance. Behold
This vile world, dust and ashes of the hopes
Of Heaven's exalted dwellers! That Creator
Whose *Let there be* made all things, today stands
Ready to annihilate them. I it was
Who drew in Europe's brain the fantasy
Of empire, I who snapped the spell of mosque,
Of church, of temple; I who taught the homeless
That all is ruled by Fate, and filled their guardians
With capitalism's hot frenzy. Who shall quench

The devouring blaze in him whose paroxysm
The fires that rage in Satan's soul have fed,
Or bow the crest of that time-weathered palm
Whose branches I have watered into greatness!

FIRST COUNSELLOR

Firm, beyond doubt, is the sovereignty of Hell.
Through it the nations have grown rotten-ripe
In slavishness: wretches, whose destiny is

ابلیس کی مجلسِ شوریٰ

۱۹۳۶ء

ابلیس

یہ عناصر کا پرانا کھیل، یہ دُنیائے دوں

ساکنانِ عرشِ اعظم کی تمناؤں کا خوں!

اس کی بربادی پہ آج آمادہ ہے وہ کارساز

جس نے اس کا نام رکھا تھا جہانِ کاف و نوں

میں نے دکھلایا فرنگی کو ملوکیت کا خواب

میں نے توڑا مسجد و دیر و کلیسا کا فسوں

میں نے ناداروں کو سکھلایا سبق تقدیر کا

میں نے منعم کو دیا سرمایہ داری کا جنوں

کون کرسکتا ہے اس کی آتشِ سوزاں کو سرد

جس کے ہنگاموں میں ہو ابلیس کا سوزِدروں

جس کی شاخیں ہوں ہماری آبیاری سے بلند

کون کرسکتا ہے اُس نخلِ کہن کو سرنگوں؟

پہلا مشیر

اس میں کیا شک ہے کہ محکم ہے یہ ابلیسی نظام

پختہ تر اس سے ہوئے خوئے غلامی میں عوام

From age to age to kneel, whose nature craves
A prostrate worship, no prayer uttered erect;
In whom no high desire can come to birth,
Or born must perish, or grow misshapenly.

From our unceasing labour this wonder blooms:
Priesthood and sainthood now are servile props
For alien dominion. Opium such as theirs
Was medicinable to Asia; had we needed,
The sophist's art lay ready, no less potent
Than droning psalm. And what if pilgrim zeal
Still shout for Mecca and the Kaaba?—blunt
Is grown the sheathless scimitar of Islam!
To whose despair stands witness that new-fangled
Canon: anathema, the Muslim who
In this age draws his sword in holy war!

SECOND COUNSELLOR

The many-headed beast bellows for power;
Is this our bane, or boon? You have not learned
What new-hatched mischiefs are about the earth.

FIRST COUNSELLOR

I have learned; but my scrutiny of the world
Assures me of no danger in what is only

ہے ازل سے ان غریبوں کے مقدر میں سجود

ان کی فطرت کا تقاضا ہے نمازِ بے قیام

آرزو اوّل تو پیدا ہو نہیں سکتی کہیں

ہو کہیں پیدا تو مرجاتی ہے یا رہتی ہے خام

یہ ہماری سعیِ پیہم کی کرامت ہے کہ آج

صوفی و مُلّا ملوکیت کے بندے ہیں تمام

طبعِ مشرق کے لیے موزوں یہی افیون تھی

ورنہ 'قوّالی' سے کچھ کم تر نہیں 'علمِ کلام!'

ہے طواف و حج کا ہنگامہ اگر باقی تو کیا

کند ہو کر رہ گئی مومن کی تیغِ بے نیام

کس کی نومیدی پہ حجّت ہے یہ فرمانِ جدید؟

'ہے جہاد اس دَور میں مردِ مسلماں پر حرام!'

دوسرا مشیر

خیر ہے سلطانئ جمہور کا غوغا کہ شر

تو جہاں کے تازہ فتنوں سے نہیں ہے باخبر!

پہلا مشیر

ہوں، مگر میری جہاں بینی بتاتی ہے مجھے

جو ملوکیت کا اک پردہ ہو، کیا اُس سے خطر!

A fig-leaf hung to hide the lust of empire.
Was it not we, when men began to observe
And to reflect, who dressed autocracy
In democratic costume? The true power
And purpose of dominion lie elsewhere,
And do not stand or fall by the existence
Of Prince or Sultan. Whether parliaments
Of nations meet, or Majesty holds court,
Whoever casts his eye on another's field
Is tyrant born. Have you not seen in the West
Those Demos-governments with rosy faces
And all within blacker than Ghengiz' soul?

THIRD COUNSELLOR

While tyranny's spirit lives on no fear should come
To trouble us! But what answer shall we give
To that accursed creature, that vile Jew,
That Prophet of no Sinai, that Messiah
Without a cross—no messenger of God,
Yet in his clasp a Book? How shall I tell you
How many a veil those godless eyes have shrivelled,
Heralding to the nations east and west
Their day of reckoning? What dire pestilence
Could outgo this! the slaves have cut the ropes
That held their lords' pavilions.

ہم نے خود شاہی کو پہنایا ہے جمہوری لباس

جب ذرا آدم ہوا ہے خود شناس و خودنگر

کاروبارِ شہریاری کی حقیقت اور ہے

یہ وجودِ میر و سلطاں پر نہیں ہے منحصر

مجلسِ ملت ہو یا پرویز کا دربار ہو

ہے وہ سلطاں، غیر کی کھیتی پہ ہو جس کی نظر

تو نے کیا دیکھا نہیں مغرب کا جمہوری نظام

چہرہ روشن، اندروں چنگیز سے تاریک تر!

تیسرا مشیر

روحِ سلطانی رہے باقی تو پھر کیا اضطراب

ہے مگر کیا اُس یہودی کی شرارت کا جواب؟

وہ کلیم بے تجلّی، وہ مسیح بے صلیب

نیست پیغبر ولیکن دربغل دارد کتاب

کیا بتاؤں کیا ہے کافر کی نگاہِ پردہ سوز

مشرق و مغرب کی قوموں کے لیے روزِ حساب!

اس سے بڑھ کر اور کیا ہوگا طبیعت کا فساد

توڑ دی بندوں نے آقاؤں کے خیموں کی طناب!

FOURTH COUNSELLOR
                    In the halls
Of mighty Rome behold the antidote.
We have revealed once more the dream of Caesar
To Caesar's offspring, whose strong arms enfold
The Italian sea and make its tumbling waves
Now soar like the pine, now like the rebeck sob!

THIRD COUNSELLOR
He!—when he casts the future, I do not trust him;
He has stripped Europe's statecraft all too naked.

FIFTH COUNSELLOR *(to Satan)*
Oh you whose fiery breath fills up the sails
Of the world! You, when it pleased you, brought to light
All mysteries; in your furnace earth and water
Became a planet panting with hot life.
We, once Heaven's simpletons, with you for teacher

Have come to knowledge, and no deeper skill
Than yours in Adam's nature has He whom men,
Poor innocents! magnify as their Preserver—
Whilst they on high whose only thought was prayer
And sanctification and the rosary

چوتھا مشیر

توڑ اس کا رومتہ الکبریٰ کے ایوانوں میں دیکھ
آلِ سیزر کو دکھایا ہم نے پھر سیزر کا خواب
کون بحرِ روم کی موجوں سے ہے لپٹا ہوا
'گاہ بالدچوں صنوبر، گاہ نالدچوں رباب'

تیسرا مشیر

میں تو اُس کی عاقبت بینی کا کچھ قائل نہیں
جس نے افرنگی سیاست کو کیا یوں بے حجاب

پانچواں مشیر
(ابلیس کو مخاطب کرکے)

اے ترے سوزِ نفس سے کارِ عالم اُستوار!
تو نے جب چاہا، کیا ہر پردگی کو آشکار
آب و گِل تیری حرارت سے جہانِ سوز و ساز
اَبلہِ جنت تری تعلیم سے دانائے کار
تجھ سے بڑھ کر فطرتِ آدم کا وہ محرم نہیں
سادہ دل بندوں میں جو مشہور ہے پروردگار
کام تھا جن کا فقط تقدیس و تسبیح و طواف

May hang their heads in everlasting shame,
Mean beside you. But though you have for vowed
Disciples all the shamans of the West,
Their wits lose credit with me. That rebel Jew,
That spirit of Mazdak come again! Not long,
And every mantle will be rent to shreds
And tatters by his fury. The desert crow
Begins to plume itself among the hawks
And eagles: dizzily the face of the world
Goes altering! What we blindly thought a handful
Of blind dust has blown whirling over the vast
Of the skies, and we see trembling, so deep sticks
The terror of tomorrow's revolution,
Mountain and meadow and the bubbling spring;—
Oh Master! on the brink of chaos lies
This earth whose sole reliance is your sceptre.

SATAN

Earth, sun and moon, celestial spheres, all realms
Of matter, lie in the hollow of my hand.
Let me once fever the blood of Europe's races,
And East and West shall see with their own eyes
A drama played out! With one incantation
I know how to drive mad their pillars of State
And princes of the Church. Tell the wise fool

تیری غیرت سے ابد تک سرنگوں و شرمسار

گرچہ ہیں تیرے مرید افرنگ کے ساحر تمام

اب مجھے ان کی فراست پر نہیں ہے اعتبار

وہ یہودی فتنہ گر، وہ روحِ مزدک کا بُروز

ہر قبا ہونے کو ہے اس کے جنوں سے تار تار

زاغِ دشتی ہو رہا ہے ہمسرِ شاہین و چرغ

کتنی سرعت سے بدلتا ہے مزاجِ روزگار

چھا گئی آشفتہ ہو کر وسعتِ افلاک پر

جس کو نادانی سے ہم سمجھے تھے اک مشتِ غبار

فتنۂ فردا کی ہیبت کا یہ عالم ہے کہ آج

کانپتے ہیں کوہسار و مرغزار و جوئبار

میرے آقا! وہ جہاں زیر و زبر ہونے کو ہے

جس جہاں کا ہے فقط تیری سیادت پر مدار

ابلیس

ہے مرے دستِ تصرف میں جہانِ رنگ و بو

کیا زمیں، کیا مہرومہ، کیا آسماں توبتو

دیکھ لیں گے اپنی آنکھوں سے تماشا غرب و شرق

میں نے جب گرما دیا اقوامِ یورپ کا لہو

کیا امامانِ سیاست، کیا کلیسا کے شیوخ

سب کو دیوانہ بناسکتی ہے میری ایک ہُو!

Who thinks our civilization fragile like
A glassblower's workshop, to destroy its cup

And flagon if he can! When Nature's hand
Has rent the seam, no needleworking logic
Of communism will put the stitches back.
I be afraid of socialists?—street-bawlers,
Ragged things, tortured brains, tormented souls!
No, if there is one monster in my path
It lurks within that people in whose ashes
Still glow the embers of an infinite hope.

Even yet, scattered among them, steadfast ones
Come forth who make lustration of their hearts
With contrite tears in the pure hour of dawn;
And he to whom the anatomy of the age
Shows clear knows well, the canker of to-morrow
Is not your communism: it is Islam.

I know its congregation is the Law's
Upholder now no more; the Muslim runs
With all the rest, makes capitalism his creed;
I know that in this dark night of the East
No shining hand that Moses raised to Pharaoh
Hides under his priest's sleeve. Yet none the less
The importunities of the hour conceal
One peril, that somewhere the Prophet's faded path
Be rediscovered. A hundred times beware,
Beware, that Prophet's ordinance, that keeps safe
The honour of women, that forges men and tries them,

کارگاہِ شیشہ جو ناداں سمجھتا ہے اسے
توڑ کر دیکھے تو اس تہذیب کے جام و سبو!
دستِ فطرت نے کیا ہے جن گریبانوں کو چاک
مزدکی کی منطق کی سوزن سے نہیں ہوتے رفو
کب ڈراسکتے ہیں مجھ کو اشتراکی کوچہ گرد
یہ پریشاں روزگار، آشفتہ مغز، آشفتہ مُو
ہے اگر مجھ کو خطر کوئی تو اُس اُمت سے ہے
جس کی خاکستر میں ہے اب تک شرار آرزو
خال خال اس قوم میں اب تک نظر آتے ہیں وہ
کرتے ہیں اشکِ سحرگاہی سے جو ظالم وضو
جانتا ہے، جس پہ روشن باطنِ ایّام ہے
مزدکیت فتنہ فردا نہیں، اسلام ہے!

جانتا ہوں میں یہ اُمت حاملِ قرآں نہیں
ہے وہی سرمایہ داری بندۂ مومن کا دیں
جانتا ہوں میں کہ مشرق کی اندھیری رات میں
بے یدِبیضا ہے پیرانِ حرم کی آستیں
عصرِ حاضر کے تقاضاؤں سے ہے لیکن یہ خوف
ہو نہ جائے آشکار! شرعِ پیغمبرؐ کہیں
الحذر! آئینِ پیغمبرؐ سے سو بار الحذر
حافظِ ناموسِ زن، مردآزما، مردآفریں

That bears a death-warrant to every shape
Of servitude, admits no Dragon Thrones,
Knows neither emperor nor roadside beggar.
It cleanses wealth of every foulness, making
The rich no more than stewards of their riches;
What mightier revolution could there be
In thought or deed than it proclaims—Earth's soil
Belongs to no earth-monarch, but to God?
And well for us if those enactments still
Lie buried snugly out of sight and mind!
Felicity it is, that the believer
Himself has lost all faith. Long may he halt
Entangled in the maze of divinity
And glozing comment on the sacred Word!

May daybreak never invade the obscure night
Of that God-meditating folk whose creed
Might burst the spells of all the finite world!
—Whether the Son of Mary perished once,
Or knew no death: whether the Attributes
Of God from God are separate or are God's
True essence: whether 'He who is to come'
Betokens the Messiah of Nazareth or
Some new Reformer clothed with Christ's own vesture:
Whether the words of Scripture are late-born
Or from eternity, and which answer holds
Salvation for the chosen People;—let
These theologian's graven images
Content the Muslim of this century!

موت کا پیغام ہر نوعِ غلامی کے لیے

نے کوئی فغفُور و خاقاں، نے فقیرِ رہ نشیں

کرتا ہے دولت کو ہر آلودگی سے پاک صاف

منعموں کو مال و دولت کا بناتا ہے امیں

اس سے بڑھ کر اور کیا فکر و عمل کا انقلاب

پادشاہوں کی نہیں، اللہ کی ہے یہ زمیں!

چشمِ عالم سے رہے پوشیدہ یہ آئیں تو خوب

یہ غنیمت ہے کہ خود مومن ہے محرومِ یقیں

ہے یہی بہتر الہیات میں اُلجھا رہے

یہ کتابُ اللہ کی تاویلات میں اُلجھا رہے

توڑ ڈالیں جس کی تکبیریں طلسمِ شش جہات

ہو نہ روشن اُس خدا اندیش کی تاریک رات

ابنِ مریم مر گیا یا زندۂ جاوید ہے؟

ہیں صفاتِ ذاتِ حق، حق سے جدا یا عینِ ذات؟

آنے والے سے مسیحِ ناصری مقصود ہے

یا مجدد جس میں ہوں فرزندِ مریم کے صفات؟

ہیں کلامِ اللہ کے الفاظ حادث یا قدیم

اُمتِ مرحوم کی ہے کس عقیدے میں نجات؟

کیا مسلماں کے لیے کافی نہیں اس دور میں

یہ الہیات کے ترشے ہوئے لات و منات؟

Keep him a stranger to the realm of action,
That on the chessboard of existence all
His pieces may be forfeit. Good, if he
Lie down in slavery till the day of doom,
Relinquishing to others what he calls
A transient globe, and hugging such belief,
Such minstrelsy, as serve to keep his eyes
Well bandaged from the theatre of life.
For yet with every breath I dread that people's
Awakening, whose religion's true behest
Is to hold watch and reckoning over all
The universe. Keep its wits bemused with dawn
Potations of its dregs of thought and prayer:
And tighten round its soul the monkish bonds!

تم اسے بیگانہ رکھو عالمِ کردار سے
تابساطِ زندگی میں اس کے سب مُہرے ہوں مات

خیر اسی میں ہے، قیامت تک رہے مومن غلام
چھوڑ کر اوروں کی خاطر یہ جہانِ بے ثبات

ہے وہی شعر و تصوف، اس کے حق میں خوب تر
جو چھپا دے اس کی آنکھوں سے تماشائے حیات

ہر نفس ڈرتا ہوں اس اُمّت کی بیداری سے میں
ہے حقیقت جس کے دیں کی احتسابِ کائنات

مست رکھو ذکر و فکرِ صبحگاہی میں اسے
پختہ تر کردو مزاجِ خانقاہی میں اسے

105. An Old Baluchi to his Son

WINDS of these wastelands be your love! Bokhara,
Delhi, are worth no more. Like running water
Go where you will: these desert plains are ours, and
        Ours are these valleys.

Honour, that high thing in a world of troubling,
Sets on the hermit's head Darius' crown. How
Glass is forged flint-hard—this strange craft they tell of
        Learn from some master!

Fortunes of States through individual prowess
Ripen, each man one star of their ascendant:
Ocean withholds her treasure when the diver
        Groping for pearlshells

Clings by land's margin. To the Muslim freedom
Gained at the price of casting off religion
Makes an ill bargain! In our world, where once more
        Civilization

Looses its wild beasts, in one more encounter
Spirit and flesh meet; on the true-believer's
Manhood God's trust lies—the machines of Europe
        Satan's alliance.

Who knows the nations' fates?—But signs abound, if
Muslims are wakeful. From your buried fathers
Ask pride of action; do not fear—*a king may*
        Smile on a beggar.

بڈھے بلوچ کی نصیحت بیٹے کو

ہو تیرے بیاباں کی ہوا تجھ کو گوارا
اس دشت سے بہتر ہے نہ دلّی، نہ بخارا

جس سمت میں چاہے صفتِ سیلِ رواں چل
وادی یہ ہماری ہے، وہ صحرا بھی ہمارا

غیرت ہے بڑی چیز جہانِ تگ و دَو میں
پہناتی ہے درویش کو تاج سردارا

حاصل کسی کامل سے یہ پوشیدہ ہنر کر
کہتے ہیں کہ شیشے کو بناسکتے ہیں خارا

افراد کے ہاتھوں میں ہے اقوام کی تقدیر
ہر فرد ہے ملّت کے مقدر کا ستارا

محروم رہا دولتِ دریا سے وہ غوّاص
کرتا نہیں جو صحبتِ ساحل سے کنارا

دیں ہاتھ سے دے کر اگر آزاد ہو ملّت
ہے ایسی تجارت میں مسلماں کا خسارا

دنیا کو ہے پھر معرکۂ روح و بدن پیش
تہذیب نے پھر اپنے درندوں کو اُبھارا

اللہ کو پامردئ مومن پہ بھروسا
ابلیس کو یورپ کی مشینوں کا سہارا

تقدیرِ اُمم کیا ہے؟ کوئی کہہ نہیں سکتا
مومن کی فراست ہو تو کافی ہے اشارا

اخلاصِ عمل مانگ نیاگانِ کہن سے
'شاہاں چہ عجب گر بنوازند گدارا!'

106. From Death to Resurrection

THE CORPSE *(to the Grave)*

WHAT thing is Resurrection?
Of what to-day the morrow?
What is it, oh my ancient chamber of sleep?

THE GRAVE
Oh hundred years dead thing,
Do you not know? It is
The secret craving all death's creatures keep.

THE CORPSE
Death in whose heart desire
Of resurrection lurks—
No death like that holds me in languishment!
Though I these hundred years
Am dead, in my dark lodging
Of dust I lie and know no discontent.
The spirit once again
To ride the jaded flesh!—
To no such resurrection my consent.

A HIDDEN VOICE
Not the wild beast nor tame,
Not snake nor scorpion, only

Nations enslaved eternal death inherit;

عالمِ برزخ

مردہ اپنی قبر سے

کیا شے ہے؟ کس امروز کا فردا ہے قیامت؟

اے میرے شبستانِ کہن! کیا ہے قیامت؟

قبر

اے مردۂ صدسالہ! تجھے کیا نہیں معلوم؟

ہر موت کا پوشیدہ تقاضا ہے قیامت!

مردہ

جس موت کا پوشیدہ تقاضا ہے قیامت

اُس موت کے پھندے میں گرفتار نہیں میں

ہر چند کہ ہوں مردۂ صدسالہ ولیکن

ظلمت کدۂ خاک سے بیزار نہیں میں

ہو روح پھر اک بار سوارِ بدنِ زار

ایسی ہے قیامت تو خریدار نہیں میں

صدائے غیب

نے نصیبِ مار و کژدم، نے نصیبِ دام و دو

ہے فقط محکوم قوموں کے لیے مرگِ ابد

No angel's trumpet-blast
Can bring those back to life
Whose bodies whilst they lived were void of spirit—
Though all that breathe are born
For the grave's long embrace,
Life's second birth no men but freemen merit.

THE GRAVE *(to the Corpse)*
Ah, villain! were you then
A thing at ease with bondage?
I did not guess what itch was in my clay!
Your carrion flesh has dyed
My darknesses more dark,
And torn earth's veil of innocence away.
Beware the carrion slave,
A hundred times beware,
Angels, and oh You Whom the worlds obey!

THE HIDDEN VOICE
Though Resurrection wrench
The fabric of existence,
It lays all mysteries bare in its fierce gale;
The earthquake that whirls hills
And peaks away like clouds
Sets the new fountain bubbling in the dale.
Each new-fledged thing proclaims
Destruction to the old,
And as their cycle runs life's barriers fail.

بانگِ اسرافیل اُن کو زندہ کرسکتی نہیں

روح سے تھا زندگی میں بھی تھی جن کا جسد

مر کے جی اُٹھنا فقط آزاد مردوں کا ہے کام

گرچہ ہر ذی روح کی منزل ہے آغوشِ لحد

قبر

(اپنے مردے سے)

آہ ظالم! تو جہاں میں بندۂ محکوم تھا

میں نہ سمجھی تھی کہ ہے کیوں خاک میری سوزناک

تیری میّت سے مری تاریکیاں تاریک تر

تیری میّت سے زمیں کا پردۂ ناموس چاک

الحذر، محکوم کی میّت سے سو بار الحذر

اے سرافیل! اے خدائے کائنات! اے جانِ پاک!

صدائے غیب

گرچہ برہم ہے قیامت سے نظامِ ہست و بود

ہیں اسی آشوب سے بے پردہ اسرارِ وجود

زلزلے سے کوہ و در اُڑتے ہیں مانندِ سحاب

زلزلے سے وادیوں میں تازہ چشموں کی نمود

ہر نئی تعمیر کو لازم ہے تخریبِ تمام

ہے اسی میں مشکلاتِ زندگانی کی کشود

THE EARTH

Oh this eternal death! this arena,
Life! Shall the storm-filled universe never
Quieten? Reason, fawning on idols,
Finds no deliverance: wisdom and folly
Bow before stocks and stones. How has man, once
Made in God's image, fallen so low?
Must such a world on heart and on spirit
Hand its load still, or why does no daybreak
Come to dispel mankind's heavy night?

زمین

آہ یہ مرگِ دوام، آہ یہ رزمِ حیات

ختم بھی ہوگی کبھی کشمکشِ کائنات!

عقل کو ملتی نہیں اپنے بتوں سے نجات!

عارف و عامی تمام بندۂ لات و منات!

خوار ہوا کس قدر آدمِ یزداں صفات!

قلب و نظر پر گراں ایسے جہاں کا ثبات!

کیوں نہیں ہوتی سحر حضرتِ انساں کی رات؟

107. A Deposed Monarch

GOOD luck to that King, cashiered so gracefully, whose
Dismissal shows how a ruling Power behaves!
In Britain's fane the King is only a plaster
Image its worshippers smash whenever they choose;
Its opiate incense is for us, the slaves—
Come, English swindler, bring out our new master!

108. Litany of the Damned

ITCHING palms, in the old old temple of Earth, have the kneelers,
    Men who remember their God only when idols are deaf.
Vain are the Hindu's rites and vain the Muhammadan's worship;
    Wailing and gnashing of teeth still are the lot of the poor.
None of earth's cities in truth is more than a populous desert,
    High though their buildings soar, kissing the sky with their
        roofs.
Axe in hand Farhad toils on;—Fate's irony witness!
    Sleek and content is Parvez, parching with drought is
        Farhad.
All that there is in that world its rulers' brains have engendered:
    Science and learning are theirs, commerce and practice of
        State;
Free of enslavement, Allah be thanked, to the huckster of
        Europe—
    Free is this country of ours, scorched in the furnace of Hell.

معزول شہنشاہ

ہو مبارک اُس شہنشاہِ نِکوفرجام کو
جس کی قربانی سے اسرارِ ملوکیت ہیں فاش
'شاہ' ہے برطانوی مندر میں اک مٹی کا بت
جس کو کر سکتے ہیں، جب چاہیں پجاری پاش پاش
ہے یہ مشک آمیز افیوں ہم غلاموں کے لیے
ساحرِ انگلیس! مارا خواجۂ دیگر تراش!

دوزخی کی مُناجات

اس دیرِ کہن میں ہیں غرض مند پجاری
رنجیدہ بتوں سے ہوں تو کرتے ہیں خدا یاد
پوجا بھی ہے بے سود، نمازیں بھی ہیں بے سود
قسمت ہے غریبوں کی وہی نالہ و فریاد
ہیں گرچہ بلندی میں عماراتِ فلک بوس
ہر شہر حقیقت میں ہے ویرانۂ آباد
تیشے کی کوئی گردشِ تقدیر تو دیکھے
سیراب ہے پرویز، جگر تشنہ ہے فرہاد
یہ علم، یہ حکمت، یہ سیاست، یہ تجارت
جو کچھ ہے، وہ ہے فکرِ ملوکانہ کی ایجاد
اللہ! ترا شکر کہ یہ خطۂ پُرسوز
سوداگرِ یورپ کی غلامی سے ہے آزاد!

109. Three Ruba'iyat

(1)

My poor estate makes proud men covetous,
Poverty such as mine ennobles us.
Beware those other rage and begging-bowls
That make the Muslim pusillanimous!

(2)

Of love and losing what words need be said?
The Self's unfolding is Life's fountain-head;
There's neither loss to ocean nor to pearl
In the pearl's loosening from the ocean's bed.

(3)

Why do no hurricanes blow about your sea?
Why is your nature without belief? Vainly
You wail against the firm decrees of God;
Why are not you yourself God's firm decree?

تین رُباعیات

(۱)

غربی میں ہوں محسودِ امیری

کہ غیرت مند ہے میری فقیری

حذر اُس فقر و درویشی سے، جس نے

مسلماں کو سکھا دی سر بزیری!

(۲)

نہ کر ذکرِ فراق و آشنائی

کہ اصلِ زندگی ہے خودنمائی

نہ دریا کا زیاں ہے، نے گہر کا

دلِ دریا سے گوہر کی جدائی

(۳)

ترے دریا میں طوفاں کیوں نہیں ہے؟

خودی تیری مسلماں کیوں نہیں ہے؟

عبث ہے شکوۂ تقدیرِ یزداں

تو خود تقدیرِ یزداں کیوں نہیں ہے؟

110. Fragments from Kashmir

(1)

KNOWN once on polished lips as Little Persia,
Downtrodden and penniless is Kashmir now;
A burning sigh breaks from the Heavens, to see
Their children crouch in awe of tyrant lords.
Telling the story of the heartless times,
An old peasant's home of misery under the hill—
Ah, this fine nation, fertile of hand and brain!
Where is Your judgment-day, oh God of ages?

(2)

The freeman's veins are firm as veins of granite;
The bondman's weak as tendrils of the vine,
And his heart too despairing and repining—
The free heart has life's tingling breath to fan it.
Quick pulse, clear vision, are the freeman's treasure;
The unfree, to kindness and affection dead,
Has no more wealth than tears of his own shedding
And those glib words he has in such good measure.

Bondman and free can never come to accord:
One is the heavens' lackey, one their lord.

کشمیر

(۱)

آج وہ کشمیر ہے محکوم و مجبور و فقیر
کل جسے اہلِ نظر کہتے تھے ایرانِ صغیر
سینئہ افلاک سے اُٹھتی ہے آہِ سوزناک
مردِ حق ہوتا ہے جب مرعوبِ سلطان و امیر
کہہ رہا ہے داستاں بیدردئ ایّام کی
کوہ کے دامن میں وہ غم خانئہ دہقانِ پیر
آہ! یہ قومِ نجیب و چرب دست و تر دماغ
ہے کہاں روزِ مکافات اے خدائے دیرگیر؟

(۲)

آزاد کی رگ سخت ہے مانندِ رگِ سنگ
محکوم کی رگ نرم ہے مانندِ رگِ تاک
محکوم کا دل مردہ و افسردہ و نومید
آزاد کا دل زندہ و پُرسوز و طرب ناک
آزاد کی دولت دلِ روشن، نفسِ گرم
محکوم کا سرمایہ فقط دیدۂ نم ناک
محکوم ہے بیگانئہ اخلاص و مروّت
ہر چند کہ منطق کی دلیلوں میں ہے چالاک
ممکن نہیں محکوم ہو آزاد کا ہمدوش
وہ بندۂ افلاک ہے، یہ خواجۂ افلاک

(3)

All of the Self dwell ignorant, whether by
Light touched or purblind. Tell us, who can, is this
    Wineshop, or Mosque? Secret our priests have
        Hidden—the shrine is herself the moth that

Round, round the shrine's lamp flutters. Credulity
Spin webs to make men think their religiousness
    Pure, unmixed with heathen delusion:
        Magic and myth are the tales alike of

Brahmin and Mullah! Grant to this country, oh
God, such a guide as hides under beggar's rags
    Prophet's high thoughts! How long shall Woolar's
        Rarest of pearls from the world lie buried?

(4)

Nations in whom life marches to action,
Waging high combat change the world's face.
Vain the astrologer's chart of tomorrow!
All his old stars have dropped from the skies.
Now the globe's centre blazes so fiercely,
Spume of the sea-waves tossed up to heaven
Hangs it with new stars; earth from her travail
Finds no release, and nature puts forth
Subtly her signs and omens, while Khizar
Wonders, by Woolar's margin, how long these
Cold Himalayan springs shall boil over!

(۳)

تمام عارف و عامی خودی سے بیگانہ
کوئی بتائے یہ مسجد ہے یا کہ میخانہ
یہ راز ہم سے چھپایا ہے میر واعظ نے
کہ خود حرم ہے چراغِ حرم کا پروانہ
طلسم بے خبری، کافری و دیں داری
حدیثِ شیخ و برہمن فسون و افسانہ
نصیب خطّہ ہو یارب وہ بندۂ درویش
کہ جس کے فقر میں انداز ہوں کلیمانہ
چھپے رہیں گے زمانے کی آنکھ سے کب تک
گہر میں آب ڈلر کے تمام یک دانہ

(۴)

دگرگوں جہاں اُن کے زورِ عمل سے
بڑے معرکے زندہ قوموں نے مارے
منجّم کی تقویمِ فردا ہے باطل
گرے آسماں سے پُرانے ستارے
ضمیرِ جہاں اس قدر آتشیں ہے
کہ دریا کی موجوں سے ٹوٹے ستارے
زمیں کو فراغت نہیں زلزلوں سے
نمایاں ہیں فطرت کے باریک اشارے
ہمالہ کے چشمے اُبلتے ہیں کب تک
خضر سوچتا ہے ڈلر کے کنارے!

(5)

I walk lonely the earth; hear my lament,
And in your breast too may these whirlwinds flame!
My grief-stained songs are precious dower; such wealth
As sad thoughts hive is rare in our world. I blame
The age for its dull wit, imagining
My labour and Farhad's long toil the same;
Far different is the noise of axe on rocks—
Listen! at my own heart the keen blade knocks.

(۵)

غریبِ شہر ہوں میں، سن تو لے مری فریاد

کہ تیرے سینے میں بھی ہوں قیامتیں آباد

مری نوائے غم آلود ہے متاعِ عزیز

جہاں میں عام نہیں دولتِ دلِ ناشاد

گلہ ہے مجھ کو زمانے کی کورذوقی سے

سمجھتا ہے مری محنت کو محنتِ فرہاد

'صدائے تیشہ کہ برسنگ میخورد دگر است

خبر بگیر کہ آوازِ تیشہ و جگر است'

PART V

PYAM-I-MASHRIQ
THE MESSAGE OF THE EAST

111. Song of the Stars

OUR nature is all the law we serve,
From all but its own rapture free,
And our long pathway's limitless curve
The gage of our immortality—
The heavens revolve at our desire; we watch and journey on.

This mansion of the senses, hall
Of idols shaped by mortal seeing,
Mêlée of being and not-being,
Storm and surge of creation, all
This realm of the hours swift-winged or slow, we watch and
        journey on.

Battlefields that war's flames have seared,
Those lunacies of subtle wits,
Thrones, diadems, and scaffolds reared
For sovereigns on whom Fortune spits,
All playthings of the ribald times, we watch and journey on.

ستاروں کا گانا

"سرودِ انجم"

هستئ ما نظام ما

مستئ ما خرام ما

گردش بی مقام ما

زندگئ دوام ما

دور فلک بکام ما، می نگریم و میرویم

جلوه که شهود را

بتکده نمود را

رزم نبود و بود را

کشمکش وجود را

عالم دیر و زود را، می نگریم و میرویم

گرمئ کارزار ها

خامئ پخته کار ها

تاج و سریر و دار ها

خواری شهریار ها

بازئ روزگار ها، می نگریم و میرویم

aster from his seat deposed,
rall set loose from slavery,
ok of Tsar and Kaiser closed,
ierce Alexander's day gone by,
Image and image-maker fled, we watch and journey on.

Man's dust so still, so turbulent,
Dwarfish of stature, giant in toil,
Now loud in roystering merriment,
Now carried shoulder-high, death's spoil,
Lord of the world and branded slave, we watch and journey on.

Like a gazelle the snare has caught,
Quivering in misery and pain,
You pant in the tangled web of thought,
Your mind plunges and gropes in vain;
From our high citadel of the skies we watch and journey on.

What is this curtain called the Apparent?
Whence do our light and darkness flow,
Or eye and heart and reason grow?
What is this nature, restless, errant,
This universe of Far and Near?—We watch and journey on.

Your vast to us is little room,
Your year our moment. You who hold
An ocean in your breast, yet whom
One dewdrop flatters!—onward rolled
In search of worlds and other worlds, we watch and journey on.

خواجہ زسروری گزشت

بندۂ زچاکری گزشت

زاری و قیصری گزشت

دور سکندری گزشت

شیوۂ بتگری گزشت، می نگریم و میرویم

خاک خموش و در خروش

ست نہاد و سخت کوش

گاہ بہ بزم ناو نوش

گاہ جنازہ ئی بدوش

میر جہان و سفتۂ گوش، می نگریم و میرویم

توبہ طلسم چون و چند

عقل تو درکشادو بند

مثل غزالہ درکمند

زاروزبون و درد مند

مابہ نشیمن بلند، می نگریم و میرویم

پردہ چہ اظہور چیست؟

اصل ظلام و نور چیست؟

چشم و دل وشعور چیست؟

فطرت ناصبور چیست؟

این ہمہ نزد و دور چیست، می نگریم و میرویم

بیش تو نزد ما کمی

سال تو پیش ماد مے

ای بکنار تو یمی

ساختہ ئی بہ شبنمی

مابہ تلاش عالمی، می نگریم و میرویم

112. God and Man

GOD

I MADE this world, from one same earth and water,
You made Tartaria, Nubia, and Iran.
I forged from dust the iron's unsullied ore,
You fashioned sword and arrowhead and gun;
You shaped the axe to hew the garden tree,
You wove the cage to hold the singing-bird.

MAN

You made the night and I the lamp,
And You the clay and I the cup;
You—desert, mountain-peak, and vale:
I—flower-bed, park, and orchard; I
Who grind a mirror out of stone,
Who brew from poison honey-drink.

محاورهٔ مابین خدا و انسان

خدا

تو ایران و تاتار و زنگ آفریدی	جہان را ز یک آب و گل آفریدم
تو شمشیر و تیر و تفنگ آفریدی	من از خاک پولاد ناب آفریدم

تبر آفریدی نہال چمن را

قفس ساختی طایر نغمۂ زن را

انسان

سفال آفریدی ایاغ آفریدم	تو شب آفریدی چراغ آفریدم
خیابان و گلزار و باغ آفریدم	بیابان و کہسار و راغ آفریدی

من آنم کہ از سنگ آئینہ سازم

من آنم کہ از زہر نوشینہ سازم

113. Solitude

I STOOD beside the ocean
  And asked the restless wave—
To what eternal troubling,
  To what quest are you slave?
With orient pearls by thousands
  Your mantle's edges shine,
But is there in you bosom
  One gem, one heart, like mine?
—It shuddered from the shore and fled,
  It fled, and did not speak.

I stood before the mountain,
  And said—Unpitying thing!
Could sorrow's lamentation
  Your hearing never wring?
If hidden in your granite
  One ruby blood-drop lie,

Do not to my affliction
  One answering word deny!
—Within its cold unbreathing self
  It shrank, and did not speak.

تنہائی

به بحر رفتم و گفتم به موج بیتابی   همیشه در طلب استی چه مشکلی داری؟

هزار نولوی لالاست در گریبانت   درون سینه چو من گوهر دلی داری؟

تپید و ازلب ساحل رمید و هیچ نگفت

به کوه رفتم و پرسیدم این چه بیدردیست؟   رسد بگوش تو آه و فغان غم زده ئی

اگر به سنگ تو لعلی ز قطرۀ خونست   یکی در آبه سخن با من ستم زده ئی

بخود خزید و نفس در کشید و هیچ نگفت

I travelled a long pathway,
     And asked the moon—Shall some
Far day, oh doomed to wander,
     Or no day, end your doom?
Our earth your silver glances
     With lakes of jasmine lace;
Is it a heart within you
     Whose hot glow sears your face?
—It stared with jealous eyes towards
     The stars, and did not speak.

Past moon and sun I journeyed,
     To where God sits enskied;—
In all Your world no atom
     Is kin of mine, I cried:
Heartless that world, this handful
     Of dust all heart, all pain;
Enchantment fills Your garden
     But I sing there in vain.
—There gathered on His lips a smile;
     He smiled, and did not speak.

رہ دراز بزیدم ز ماہ پرسیدم   سفرنصیب،نصیب تو منزلی است کہ نیست

جہان ز پرتو سیمای تو سمن زاری   فروغ داغ تو از جلوهٔ دلی است کہ نیست

سوی ستارہ رقیبانہ دید و ہیچ نگفت

شدم بحضرت یزدان گذشتم از مہ و مہر   کہ در جہان تو یک ذرہ آشنایم نیست

جہان تہی ز دل ومشت خاک من ہمہ دل   چمن خوش است ولی درخور نوایم نیست

تبسمی بلب او رسید و ہیچ نگفت

114. Houri and Poet
(In reply to a poem of Goethe)

HOURI

THE red wine you leave untested, and your eyes do not come
near me;
It is strange you know so little of love's fashions and love's
biddings!
In each breath you draw the fever of some endless quest is
burning,
In each song you sing the fire of some long passion's hope is
glowing;
With these songs you have created such a world of bliss, that
round me
As if called by incantation I see paradise unfolding.

POET

You beguile the wanderer's fancy with these words that prick
the senses,
But the thorn-pricks of the desert are the joy that he exults in.
Can I help it if my nature love no dwelling, if my spirit
Be as fitful as the dawn-breeze when it flutters through the
tulips?
While a mistress stands before me and her loveliness enchants me,
Even then my thoughts are pining for a mistress yet more lovely;
In a spark I crave a star, and in a star a sun: my journey
Has no bourn, no place of halting: it is death to me to linger.
When I lift the winecup brimming with the nectar of one
springtime,
A desire of unborn springtides comes awake to change my
music,
And with eyes full of unrest, with inextinguishable longing,
I go seeking the fulfilment of what cannot know fulfilment.
For the heart of lovers wither in interminable heavens
With no pain for them for sharing, neither heartache nor heart-
comfort.

حور و شاعر

(در جواب نظم کوتہ موسوم بہ حور و شاعر)

حور

عجب اینکہ تو ندانی رہ ورسم آشنائے	نہ بہ بادہ میل داری نہ بہ من نظر کشائے
نفسی کہ میکدازی غزلی کہ می سرائے	ہمہ ساز جستجوئی ہمہ سوز آرزوئے

بہ نوای آفریدی چہ جہان دلگشائے

کہ ارم بہ چشم آید چو طلسم سیمیائے

شاعر

مگر اینکہ لذت او نرسد نوک خاری	دل رہروان فریبی بہ کلام نیش داری
دل ناصبور دارم چو صبا بہ لالہ زاری	چکنم کہ فطرت من بہ مقام در نسازد
تپد آن زمان دل من پی خوبتر نگاری	چو نظر قرار گیرد بہ نگار خوبروئے
سرمنزلی ندارم کہ بمیرم از قراری	ز شرر ستارہ جویم ز ستارہ آفتابی
غزلی دگر سرایم بہ ہوای نوبہاری	چو ز بادۂ بہاری قدحی کشیدہ خیزم
بہ نگاہ ناشکیبی بہ دل امیدواری	طلبم نہایت آن کہ نہایتی ندارد

دل عاشقان بمیرد بہ بہشت جاودانی

نہ نوای دردمندی نہ غمی نہ غمگساری

115. Life and Strife
(In reply to a poem of Heine)

'LONG years were mine', said the sea-shattered cliff,
'Yet never taught me what is this called *I*.'
A headlong-hurrying wave cried: 'Only if
I move I live, for if I halt I die.'

116. Slavery

MAN let himself, dull thing, be wooed
By his own kind to servitude,
And cast the dearest pearl he had
Before Jamshed and Kaikobad;
Till so ingrained his cringings were,
He grew more abject than a cur—
Who ever saw at one dog's frown
Another dog's meek head bow down?

زندگی و عمل

(درجواب نظم ہانیہ موسوم بہ سوالات)

ساحل افتادہ گفت گرچہ بسی زیستیم هيچ نہ معلوم شد آہ کہ من چیستم

موج زخود رفتہ ئی تیز خرامید و گفت هستم اگر میروم گر نروم نیستم

غلامی

آدم از بی بصری بندگی آدم کرد گوہری داشت ولی نذر قباد و جم کرد

یعنی از خوی غلامی ز سگان خوار تر است من ندیدم کہ سگی پیش سگی سر خم کرد

117. Quatrain

SWEET is the time of Spring, the red Rose cried;
Sweeter an hour here than an age outside;
Before some lover plucks you for his cap,
Sweetest to die in this green garden's lap.

118. Epilogue

WHEN, to leave earth, I gathered what was mine,
To have known me through and through was each man's claim;
But of this traveller none knew truly what he
Spoke, or to whom he spoke, or whence he came.

رباعی

گل گفت کہ عیش نو بہاری خوشتر   یک صبح چمن ز روزگاری خوشتر

زان پیش کہ کس ترابد پستار زند

مردن بکنار شاخساری خوشتر

اختتامیہ

چورخت خویش بر بستم ازین خاک   ہمہ گفتند باما آشنا بود

ولیکن کس مدانست این مسافر

چہ گفت و با کہ گفت و از کجا بود

NOTES

(In these notes the numbers are those of the poems. Sentences in brackets with the initials 'N.A.' have been contributed by Dr. Nazir Ahmad Shah. For further biographical and other detail see *Encyclopaedia of Islam*; *Handwoerterbuch des Islam; Encyclopaedia of Religion and Ethics;* E.G. Browne, *A Literary History of Persia;* T.G. Bailey, *Urdu Literature.*)

Bāng-i-darā. The bugle or other signal for the caravan to begin the day's march.

1. The last four lines are in the original a Persian couplet. Here and throughout I have italicized such lines to indicate that Iqbal is quoting from another poet. Quite often he inserts Persian lines of his own in Urdu poems. (This practice, which had been known earlier, was made into a popular fashion thirty or forty years ago, chiefly by patriotic poets endeavouring to awaken the Muslims of India. They found that their audiences relished a sprinkling of Persian lines, and of Persian and Quranic quotations brought in for emphasis at the end of passages. The practice has now more or less been dropped, which is not to be regretted. It had a parallel in the prose style popularized by Abul Kalam Azad.– N.A.)

3. *The Sun.* The title of Surah xci of the Quran.

4. *Kalīm.* Mīrzā Abu Tālib of Hamadhān was a Persian Court-poet of Mughal India, who died in 1652.

   The Shias. The Shī'a sect, widespread in Islam and particularly in Persia, but viewed as heretical by the Sunni majority, pays special reverence to 'Alī, cousin and son-in-law of Muhammad (PBUH) and, as Khalīfa (Caliph), his fourth successor.

   Vendors-of-beauty. The hereditary prostitutes of the Tibbi quarter of Lahore are at the same time singers, and a kind of professional symbiosis may be said to exist between them and the poets, who often write songs to be sung by them, to their mutual advantage. A respectable citizen may make an occasional evening excursion to Tibbi, to hear some music in company, but he should not go often. A poet enjoys a certain customary licence.

   Mansur. See note to no. 26, where 'the Mystic' refers to this man.

7. The diction of this poem is a blend of Urdu and Hindi, suited to the theme of Muslim-Hindu friendship.

8. *Those towers.* The great mausoleum of the emperor Jehāngīr, which stands on the other side of the Rāvi from the old walled city of Lahore.

13. *A dimple.* In Urdu a *mole*—a word less poetical in English, as well as somewhat ambiguous in this context.

The nightingale-voice. The Persian poet Sādī, in the thirteenth century, when the Mongols were ravaging western Asia.

Dagh. 'Dāgh' was the pen-name of Mīrzā Khān, an eminent Urdu poet born in 1831, who retired from Delhi in the final decay of the Mughal Court there, and died at Hyderabad in 1904. Iqbal in youth received some tuition in versification from him.

Ibn Badrūn. He flourished in Spain about 1200, and wrote a commentary on a poem by Ibn 'Abdūn (d.1134) on the fall of the Aftasid dynasty there.

16. (This poem, inspired by Italy's attack on Turkey and her seizure of Tripoli in 1911, was recited by Iqbal in that year in the Bādshāhī Masjid, or Imperial Mosque, of Lahore. In those days well-known personages would often address the congregation here after Friday prayers, from the outer pulpit; partly because the place protected them against interference by the police. On this occasion, I learn from the distinguished writer of Lahore, Mr Muhammad Aslam, a friend of Iqbal, about a thousand people were present; many of them, and the poet himself, were in tears.— N.A.)

Suppliant knee. Lit., the *sijdah*, or kneeling and touching the forehead to the ground, a part of the daily ritual of prayer. Iqbal very frequently refers to it in order to epitomize a humility which, by itself, he thinks an abject kind of religion.

17. *Moses, Abraham.* These characters, so often invoked by Iqbal, wear more poetical names in Urdu, as Kalim, 'the speaker' (he who talked with God), and Khalīl, 'the friend' (of God).

Alexander. 'Sikandar' is usually for Iqbal the embodiment of senseless aggression and brutal conquest, instead of the romantic hero of Eastern folk-lore.

Tyrants and flames. Iqbal refers, as often, to Nimrod, of whom there are many Muslim legends. He tried to burn Abraham at the stake, but his victim was miraculously preserved. Here Nimrod represents British imperialism.

Of Kings. Surah lxvii of the Quran has the title 'Sovereignty'.

Mahmud, Ayaz. Ayāz was the favourite slave of Mahmūd, the conquering ruler of Ghaznī (969-1030); their relationship is often referred to by Iqbal as discreditable to both.

Jamshed. Like Alexander, the old Persian ruler stands here for the dead hand of the past, with its brutish conquerors trampling upon mankind.

Gabriel's Wing. Iqbal chooses this Archangel to typify inspiration because in the Quran it is he who reveals God's mysteries and messages to mankind, and in particular to Muhammad (PBUH).

Ghazal. These seventeen ghazals are taken from a collection of nearly seventy, in two series, forming the first half of the volume. Nos. 1 to 7 in the English correspond with nos. 2, 4, 7, 8, 10, 11, 16 of the first series in the Urdu. Nos. 8 to 17 in the English correspond with nos. 1, 4, 7, 16, 30, 31, 40, 49, 50, 61 of the second.—The ghazal is traditionally a light love-poem; Iqbal, more than perhaps any other poet, uses it as a vehicle for serious ideas. Its peculiarity is that its couplets, strung together by the rhyme like beads on a string, may have no real connection of thought; or the connection may derive from some unity of feeling not apparent on the surface. In other poems, too, the same rhyme-scheme is often associated with the same loose construction. In the ghazals translated here I have left a gap between each pair of lines in those where the discontinuity seems greatest.

19. *Eternity.* (*Lā-makān*, 'not-space'; the phrase is Arabic, but the concept is Persian. It can mean God here it suggests infinity of time and space, or what is outside time and space; the eternity before and after Man; or the world of angels, whose natures suffer from no contradictions.—N.A.)

How could an Angel. When the angels were ordered by God to pay homage to new-created Adam, Satan refused. (Quran xviii. 51.)

Their gracious words. (Lit., 'But is this sweet word Your interpreter or mine?' The couplet is obscure and difficult, but appears to signify that Gabriel, Muhammad (PBUH) and the Quran, while claimed by God as His own, really reveal the nature of *Man*, who is the measure of all things. Iqbal approaches at times, though guardedly, an idea of God as contained or encompassed in the mind that contemplates Him. Throughout this poem he is writing in his mood of defiance; each couplet in turn dwells on some imperfection in the work of creation. N.A.)

21. *Saqi.* The 'Sāqī' was originally the page or cupbearer of the Arabs, then the hetaira of the Persians, the mistress who pours the wine. Wine symbolizing truth or inspiration, the Sāqī came to be the filler of the spiritual cup, and hence the religious leader or guide, or even God. In poetry there is often an intentional ambiguity.

Rumi. Jalāl ul-Dīn Rūmī (1207-1273), the great Persian poet of the Sufi or mystical tradition, represents for Iqbal the highest possible reach of inspiration or insight.

Parvez. Iqbal has very many allusions to the legend of Khosrau Parvēz, King of Persia 590-627, through whose tyranny the builder

Farhād was compelled to cut a way through a mountain with his axe in the vain hope of winning his lover Shīrīn. Often Iqbal makes Parvēz stand for the rich man oppressing the poor, or the powerful nation attacking the weak; while Farhād represents the oppressed, or the proletariat, or patient merit spurned by the unworthy. He seldom refers to Shīrīn.

22. *India's wineshops.* The wineshop or tavern figures in poetry as the source of personal, vital, or mystical religion, in contrast with the more formal and external religion of the church.

23. *Father's glance.* In Sufi lore the inspired man of religion has a mysteriously compelling and transforming glance.

26. In an introductory note to the poem Iqbal explains that he wrote down 'these few scattered thoughts' in memory of a visit in 1933 (he had gone to Afghanistan to advise on education) to the tomb of Sanā'ī, and that he borrowed the metre of a famous *qasīda* written by the latter. Sanā'ī was a poet who flourished about 1100 at the later Ghaznavid court, was converted to a religious life, and became a prominent Sufi. (The Persian quotation at the close of Iqbal's note, 'We come following in the footsteps of Sanā'ī and 'Attār', is from Rūmī, with whom Iqbal thus puts himself, a little audaciously perhaps, on a footing of equality.— N.A.)

My madness. Janūn, a constantly recurring term, is the 'madness' of the lover or worshipper in a state of rapture, or of the poet in his inspired fit. (Poets and lovers conventionally suffer from madness which can only be allayed by long wanderings in wildernesses, and the intensity of their affliction is measured by the size of desert required to soothe it. Here Iqbal has betaken himself to the ultimate wilderness, the entire cosmos, but this has done nothing to cure his malady which, he now realizes, can only be overcome by development of the Self.—N.A.)

Not unknown to Ocean. The ocean is the Infinite, or God, whose waves are finite human souls.

The Mystic. Al-Hallāj, 'the carder', was a Persian mystic who was imprisoned for heresy on the ground that he identified the individual soul and the divine spirit, and was tortured to death at Baghdād in 922. Iqbal discusses him in the fourth of his lectures on *the Reconstruction of Religious Thought in Islam.*

That Archangel. 'Isrāfīl'; an angel of immense stature, who holds a trumpet to his mouth ready to blow it as soon as God gives the signal for the Day of Judgment.

Is Doomsday far. A quotation from Sanā'ī; lit., 'The Chinese have put on the pilgrim's robe, the Meccan is asleep in Batḥa' (the valley of Mecca).

The bowl of faith...the wine of No. In the text we have 'the goblet of *illā*' and 'the wine of *lā*', these being the Arabic *except* and *no* in the ritual phrase 'there is no god but God.'

The Frankish glassblowers. Firangī (Firang, Firangistān) is a term habitually used by Urdu poets for 'European' or 'Western' when a tone of hostility or contempt is implied. I have sometimes rendered the word by 'European', 'white man', etc.

Like Moses. Moses, threatened by Pharaoh, was told by God to draw his hand out from under his sleeve, shining with a mysterious light; Quran xx. 22, and cp. Exodus iv. 6, where Moses' hand is made 'leprous as snow'.

Myself bound fast. This line, Iqbal points out in a note, is slightly altered from one by Sā'ib, a Persian poet born in 1603 who made a long stay in India.

Chapter, and Word, and Book. Lit., 'He the Quran, he the Scripture, he the Y.S., he the T.H.' Several Surahs of the Quran are preceded by enigmatic groups of letters; these are xxxvi and xx.

28. *Rāj.* This it may be hoped is a familiar enough word to be used in English: it means 'sovereignty', and in particular the British power in India.

Hindu and Muslim fight. Lit., 'I have not seen Shaikh and Brahmin'—the intolerant leaders of the rival religions.

29. *One bold heart.* Lit., 'A hundred thousand scholars head-in-collar, one Moses head-on-hand' (carrying his life in his hand).

Fear not! Arabic in the original, as usual with Quranic fragments (this is from xx. 71), somewhat as Dante mixes fragments of Latin with his Italian.

34. (One of Iqbal's greatest ghazals; it has a quality found in none of its predecessors. He is, I think, prophesying the coming of a new civilization, a Kingdom of God on earth; one that will be, as the term is usually understood, 'socialistic', but with an additional and more spiritual element of *charity*. In the successive couplets he seems to define the Kingdom, negatively, as the mystic defines God with his 'Not thus, not thus—'; he excludes from it in turn the frivolous devotees of Westernism, the narrow-minded philosopher, the fanatic, the plutocrat, the passive and irresolute.—N.A.)

Kūfa. A leading city of the early Arab conquerors, founded by them on the Euphrates in the seventh century.

The fleshpots. In the original of this couplet the contrast is again between Parvēz and Farhād.

Mahatmas. In the original, 'the Rishi'—*Rishis* being the philosophers and teachers of ancient India. Iqbal clearly has in mind Mahatma Gandhi and his efforts to purge orthodox Hinduism of its abuses, especially its treatment of 'untouchables'.

35. *Turkey*. That is, the Westernizing, un-Islamic Turkey of Mustafa Kemal.
36. A *rubāʿī* is a quatrain rhymed AABA. These six are taken from pages 14, 116, 117, 119 and 120 of *Bāl-i-Jibrīl*.
37. Iqbal visited the Mosque of Cordoba during his European tour of 1931-2; in Anwar Beg's book can be seen a photograph of him at prayer there. He wrote several poems at this time on Arab Spain.

Love. Throughout the translation of this poem 'Love' is used, for want of a better word, for *ʿishq*, which normally has this meaning, but which for Iqbal has a very wide sense and plays a large part in his philosophy: it is creative passion, high emotion, divine spark, enthusiasm for an ideal, ardent self-dedication, or the force that drives the individual to realize himself through wrestlings with the world and with God.

The heart's warm blood. Urdu avoids monotony by having several words for 'heart', and also by making play with the *liver*, the word used here—*jigar*; co. Latin *jecur,* with the same poetical use. (Persian and Urdu poets distinguish, though not strictly, between heart and liver as seats of emotion. To the former belongs passionate love; to the latter a more placid affection—one's child, for instance, is 'a corner of one's liver'. In matters of art, such as this passage is concerned with, the heart is the source of inspiration, while the liver or its blood helps to sustain the effort of creation; and poets 'burn the blood of their liver' in the same way as in Europe they burn the midnight oil.—N.A.)

Rome's chief daughter. One would like to suppose that Iqbal was alluding to the Italian Renaissance, but if so it is odd that he should put it after the Protestant Reformation and the French Revolution. Conceivably he was thinking of the Risorgimento; but his readers have often taken these lines to refer to the 'new Italy' of Mussolini, by which Iqbal was for a moment favourably impressed.

Guadalquivir. From *Wādī al-Kabīr*, 'the great valley'.
40. *Virgins of heaven*. It should be unnecessary to remark that the educated Muslim, nowadays at any rate, understands these *houris* in a purely figurative sense.
41. The title is an Arabic phrase.
44. This poem contains seven sections; I have omitted the fourth, fifth and sixth, which are inclined to wander into the no-man's-land between poetry and philosophy.

Sacred thread. The distinguishing mark of the caste Hindu, and for Iqbal a symbol of idolatry.
The Sufi. The Sufis represented in Islamic history the element of mystical or personally experienced religion (as distinct from formal theology or ritual), the element always emphasized by Iqbal. In India the Sufis, grouped in monastic Orders, had done much missionary work, and learned something for the Hindus among whom they worked. Like the analogous Bhakti movement in medieval Hinduism, and various mystical

movements in Christendom, Sufism had often been tinged by a kind of social radicalism or anti-feudalism. (See A.J. Arberry, *Sufism*, 1950; H.A.R. Gibb, *Muhammadanism*, 1953, chap. 8.)

Siddīq. 'The Truthful'—Abū Bakr, the first Caliph.

So may Fate... (The poet invokes a blessing on God, or at least on God's creation, before imploring His gifts, in the phraseology of the beggar who calls down blessings on the passer-by before asking for alms.—N.A.)

Mahmud's pomp. The reference is again to Mahmūd of Ghaznī and his slave Ayāz.

My wings. (The final couplet is borrowed from a Persian poem describing the Prophet's ascent into Heaven. He was being guided by Gabriel, as Dante was by Virgil, but before the ultimate vision was attained Gabriel confessed the impossibility for him of going any further: the last ascent was for the Prophet alone.—N.A.)

45. *It shall not serve them.* (The original of this line is very obscure. It *may* mean rather: European imperialism, by its control of sea and air, creates a kind of whirlpool by which to destroy us, and which we ignorant victims mistake for unalterable fate.—N.A.)

46. Satan is here, as usually by Iqbal, called *Iblīs*, a word derived apparently from *diabolos*. In this and various other poems Satan is not pure evil, as he is in no. 104, but embodies the spirit of denial and rebellion that is, for Iqbal, a part of the motive force of history and human development.

That rent robe. This *chāk-i-dāman*, the tearing of the bosom of the dress under passionate emotion, occurs incessantly in poetry. In Satan's case it was the perverse excitement of his first act of disobedience, which is referred to in the next couplet also.

All hope renounce... Lit., 'despair, or despair not'; the reference is to the Quran, xxxix. 53, 'Despair not of the mercy of God'.

Your ministers... Lit., 'Khizar is without hand and foot (powerless), Elias too is without hand and foot.'

50. *Alwand.* A mountain in Media, with which many legends are connected.

Then since at last. (The last stanza is in the original a celebrated Persian couplet from a ghazal of Ḥāfiz.—N.A.)

51. *One creed and one world.* (*Tauḥid*, 'the unity of the Godhead' here seems to imply also harmony among men. There is an allusion in this and the previous couplet to the situation in the Panjab under the Unionist Party led by Sir Fazl-i-Husain. The tactics of this oddly-named party consisted in playing off Muslim against Hindu, and, within the Muslim fold, 'agriculturist' against 'non-agriculturist'; this involved an appeal to old local or 'tribal' customs of inheritance, as opposed to Islamic law. Iqbal, who had no high opinion of the Unionists, mostly feudal landlords, is protesting against these tactics; he did the same in a speech of 1935.–N.A.)

52. Nādir Shāh (1880-1933) seized the throne of Afghanistan in 1929, after the fall of Amanullah. Iqbal had high hopes of these two men in turn, as possible creators of an ideal Islamic polity. Nādir was murdered just after Iqbal's visit to him in 1933. (The 'cloud' represents Nādir himself, and the 'pearls' bestowed on him by God as a parting gift become 'rain', and then 'tears', as the poem proceeds. The last couplet, Persian in the original, implies that Nādir's presence in Afghanistan will impart to its people a fresh and undying inspiration. The 'poppy' stands, as often, for the *millat-i-Islām*, or Muslim community; the evolution of this symbol in Iqbal's work has been the subject of a study by Abid Ali Abid. The Persian word *lāla* means poppy or tulip; it is usually rendered in English translation of poetry as tulip, but neither of the two Indian species of tulip exactly fits the conventional description of *lāla*. It is probable that in our poets' minds the two flowers are not so nicely discriminated as they would be by English writers.—N.A.)

53. *Turania's peoples*. Tūrān, or Turania, is a general term for Muslim central Asia, eastward from Iran with which it is often contrasted. There is an echo in this poem of the 'Pan-Turanian' movement which had a certain vogue in the days of the Young Turks. Their leader, Enver Bey, was for a time one of Iqbal's hopes; and the introduction of Tīmūr, or Tamberlane, is another example of Iqbal's lifelong search for heroes.

55. A *Pīr* is a Muslim saint, or spiritual guide; but in some backward areas of the western Panjab a class of hereditary *pīrs*, trading on the ignorance and superstition of the masses, has accumulated great wealth and power. Iqbal is condemning a cult that has nothing in common with pure Islamic practice.

The reformer. The Shaikh-i-Mujaddid, or religious reformer, of this poem was Shaikh Ahmad of Sirhind, north of Delhi, who was born in 1564. He defied, but was later taken into favour by, the Emperor Jehangir. See, on his teachings, S.A. Vahid, *Iqbal*, pp. 105-8.

Five Rivers. This is the meaning of 'Panjāb'.

57. In one of his speeches Iqbal told an anecdote of how Satan's disciples were surprised one day to find him lounging in an armchair over a cigar; he explained that he was now at leisure, having handed over charge of his affairs to the British government.

59. *Brahmins*. Lit., 'Brahmins of the Ka'aba': that is, the worldly *pīrs* whose cult is no better than idolatry.

The Rod of Moses. Lit., 'Moses' blow': the allusion is to his striking the rock and making water gush forth.

64. Adapted, Iqbal says in a note, from Mohī ul-Dīn ibn 'Arabī—a Spanish mystic whose pantheistic leanings Iqbal elsewhere controverted.

73. Damascus was bombarded by the French in 1925, in the course of their efforts to make good their hold on Syria. They bombarded it again in 1945, to signalize the liberation of France from the Nazis.

79. *Barmecidal invitation.* A Persian proverbial expression, meaning to tilt the flask, as if pouring wine for a guest, without in fact pouring any.

81. This and the next poem (and no. 103) refer to the partial concessions made to nationalism in India in the years following the Great War, when the Provinces were allowed to choose Ministries for themselves, with limited powers. Iqbal agreed with most of the thoroughgoing nationalists in viewing these concessions as a mere sham.

85. *Baals and Dagons.* In the original, 'Lāt and Manāt': these were idols of pagan times in Arabia. (See Quran, Surah liii.)

87. *Ataturk or Reza Shah.* Mustafa Kemal of Turkey, and the founder (in 1925) of the Pahlavi dynasty in Persia; both westernizers, and hence unacceptable to Iqbal.

88. *One sole Archfiend.* Iblīs, or Satan, had been made by God out of fire: this was one of his motives for refusing to kneel to Adam, who was made out of dust.

91. *Khutan's meadows.* Khūtān, part of eastern Turkestan, was conquered by Islam in the early eleventh century; musk-deer are often associated with it in poetry.

95. *Heath and sand.* This is a guess at the meaning of *chōb-i-nai*, a very obscure phrase.

99. *Aleppo's rare glass.* Aleppo (Ḥalab) was traditionally a glass-working centre.

101. The incident occurred, says Iqbal, when a delegation of the Turkish Red Crescent visited Lahore.

104. *Let there be.* Lit., 'the world of K and N', alluding to the Arabic phrase *kun fikān*: '(God said) be, and it was.'

   Droning psalm. (*Qawwālī* is the religious singing allowed by the Sufis under certain restrictions, music in general having no place in Muslim worship; Iqbal here regards it as an enervating or demoralizing influence.—N.A.)

   That vile Jew. Karl Marx.

   Caesar's offspring. Mussolini.

   Now soar like the pine. The line is a Persian quotation, whose precise import is hard to make out.

   Mazdak. Mazdak lived in Persia about A.D. 500, and was the chief protagonist of a cult, founded two centuries earlier, which proposed to eradicate the causes of hatred among men by allowing property and women to be enjoyed in common. He gained influence under King Kawadh, but his doctrines were disliked by the rich, and after a political upheaval he and his followers were massacred. Later in the poem Iqbal uses *Mazdaki* and *Mazdakiyat* for 'communistic' and 'communism'.

Makes capitalism his creed. The Quranic prohibition (similar to that of all Christian Churches until recent times) of interest on loans makes capitalism incompatible with Islam.

The Son of Mary. (Most Muslims hold that Jesus was not crucified, but that some other person was executed in his place; Jesus was taken up into the fourth heaven, which in Persian and Urdu poetry is always his abode.—N.A.)

106. *Wild beast nor tame.* Or, 'neither beast nor insect'.

Angels, and oh you... Lit., 'Oh Isrāfīl, oh God of the universe, oh pure spirit!'—The last phrase meaning Gabriel.

107. The ruler is Edward VIII.

110. These pieces, which Iqbal—who had Kashmiri ancestry—introduces under a fanciful Kashmiri nom-de-plume assumed for the occasion, number nineteen in the original; the five here translated are numbers 3, 10, 11, 12 and 19.

Woolar. A lake in Kashmir, amid beautiful hills and forests.

Far different... (A Persian couplet by Mīrzā Jānjānān Maẓhar, a Sufi poet born in central India and murdered at Delhi by a religious fanatic in 1780.—N.A.)

111. *Your mind...* Lit., 'Your intellect is (busy) in opening-and-closing.'

114. The whole scheme of this volume was suggested by Goethe's *Westoestlicher Diwan.*

117. (Iqbal had a spirit of contradiction in him—even his grand doctrine of 'Selfhood' was inspired in part by a wish to contradict the old Sufis, in the same way as Nietzsche wanted to go against Schopenhauer. These verses were, I think, meant as a retort to a well-known, and far more poetical, quatrain by Zēbunnissa, daughter of the Emperor Aurangzēb, who for political reasons prevented her from marrying:— 'Let that hand be cut off that has not hung about the neck of a beloved....'—N.A.)

118. This Persian quatrain is taken from p. 199 of *Armaghān-i-Hejāz.*